PARADISE ON EARTH

Some Thoughts on European Images of
Non-European Man

by HENRI BAUDET

Translated by Elizabeth Wentholt

New Haven and London, Yale University Press, 1965

Library of Congress catalog card number: 65-11174

Published with assistance from the foundation
established in memory of
Henry Weldon Barnes of the Class of 1882,
Yale College.

Translated from the original Dutch
Het Paradijs op Aarde,
published in The Netherlands by
Royal Van Gorcum Ltd., 1959

FOREWORD

This provocative little book, first published in Dutch in 1959 and now translated into English for the first time, is both timely and original. It is timely in the sense that it deals with a theme of enormous contemporary interest, namely the "relation of European man to non-European man" or, more precisely, the attitudes of Europeans toward the non-Western and "colonial" peoples through the centuries. As the author, a member of the history faculty of the University of Groningen, reminds us, there has been a complete reversal in the relations between the Western and non-Western worlds in our time. Europe, once queen of the world, has beaten a hasty retreat from Asia and Africa. The era of classic expansion is over. At such a time, what more natural—or more important—than for a historian to ask what Europeans have thought about non-Europeans, and for what reasons. It is in this question, and in the answers given to it, that the originality of this book lies. It is a book about ideas rather than "facts." Hitherto, historians have devoted themselves mainly to the military, political, and economic facts of the relationship. Baudet, however, addresses himself to "the other relationship" which reigns in the minds of men. "Its domain is that of the imagination, of all sorts of images of non-Western people and worlds which have flourished in our [European] culture, images which are derived not from observation, experience and perceptible reality but from a psychological urge."

The range of Professor Baudet's scholarship is impressive. He begins with the birth of Europe in the "Mediterranean era" and works down to the present century. Throughout this long period he notes a fundamental ambivalence in the European's feelings toward non-Western peoples. On the one hand is his feeling, first expressed by the Greeks and later exhibited in the urge to expansion, of superiority and hostility to the "barbarians." On the other hand he compares himself unfavorably to certain non-European types, discovers in them qualities which he very much admires and finds lacking in himself and his own civilization. Baudet relates this latter feeling of modesty, and even of inferiority and guilt, to the age-old myth of man's fall from "Paradise." The European longs for his lost purity and looks for it in a far-distant time or place.

Two things impress about the historical fortunes of this myth. The first is its persistence and pervasiveness throughout the period of Western expansion. Except for the nineteenth century, when Europeans assessed their own culture more positively, exoticism continued to increase and flourish. Paradoxically, at the same time that Europe was conquering the world, Europeans were peopling that world with noble savages and/or sages of superior insight and wisdom. The second striking thing about the myth is its successive identification with different peoples and places. It is fascinating to follow its permutations. During the Middle Ages when Christendom confronted Islam, Europeans canonized *le bon nègre,* believed to be Christian and to inhabit the ancient Christian kingdom of Ethiopia. In the "Atlantic era" the noble savage moved west and changed color. The American Indian displaced the Negro as the paragon. Though a pagan and though in fact often exploited by the European invader, the Indian was clothed with all the attributes which man had supposedly possessed in Paradise before the Fall: natural goodness, innocence, and physical beauty, freedom from the wickedness and suffering of "civilization." There was a further reshuffling of images in the eighteenth century. Now the noble Oriental hove into sight and took his place beside the primitive Indian. China, revealed to Europe by the Jesuits, became for many the land of perfect

vi

peace, of exquisite artistic taste and ethical wisdom. Likewise, the Muslim, once feared and detested, became the champion of a noble and logical religion, tolerant by comparison with an "infamous" Christianity.

So in the end this turns out to be a study in changing European taste and self-criticism, especially the latter. The European's images of non-European man are not primarily if at all descriptions of real people, but rather projections of his own nostalgia and feeling of inadequacy. They are judgments on himself and his history. The outsider, whether primitive or civilized, is held up as a model of what he (the European) had been in happier days, or of what he would like to be and perhaps could be once again.

Professor Baudet's book has still wider implications. It might be said to be a case study of the ambivalence which perhaps runs through all cultures: the conviction of righteousness and superiority combined with profound self-doubt. Is this not true, for instance, of American culture? With respect to this ambivalence Baudet proffers a challenging hypothesis. The more a culture is "historically orientated," i.e., the more it is satisfied with its own historical achievement, as in nineteenth-century Europe, the less it will be inclined "to seek Paradise beyond the horizon." By a like token, however, the more it develops a "protesting attitude" toward history, as in the eighteenth century, the more it will be attracted to the outside world, the more it will invest the latter with ideal attributes. "Nostalgia," the author concludes, "was not wholly foreign to any period [of European history], but it tended to be more dominant in some than in others."

FRANKLIN L. BAUMER

Yale University
May 1965

PREFACE

I present this book to its readers as an introduction to a problem that has concerned me since my personal experience brought me into close touch with the postwar process of de-colonization—a process that took barely fifteen years to change our world completely. Even more interesting than the changes themselves, it seemed to me, were the ways in which the Euro-pean mind succeeded in adapting to them. Being European myself, I have tried to analyze the psychological elements in our complicated European personality that seemed to me to play decisive roles in our reaction to this enormous and ineluctable problem, for which we were in many respects badly prepared. To what experience, what past, what fundamental beliefs could Europe appeal in making the mental adjustments required by the new era?

That is precisely what this small book is about. It looks into only one aspect—albeit an important one—of a many-sided dilemma. In discussing European images of non-European man from the birth of Europe to the beginning of the present century, it sets the stage for our present predicament. In the not-too-distant future I hope to complete a second volume concerning our own twentieth century.

I feel particularly thankful to George Pierson, to Harry Benda, and to Marian Neal Ash for all they did to have this book published in America. The occasion it gives me to thank them here for their precious help and their friendship is for me one of the great pleasures of its appearance.

HENRI BAUDET

Groningen, The Netherlands
March 1965

CONTENTS

*L'Orient s'avance, invincible, fatal aux
dieux de la lumière, par le charme du
rêve, par la magie du clair-obscur.*

MICHELET

I

Thirty centuries ago, on the shores of the Mediterranean, Europe was born. For a vast stretch of time it had been nothing more than a geographical concept, a promontory, an outpost of the continent of Asia: Cap d'Asie, as Valéry said. No concept, no consciousness, no definition distinguished West from East until, three thousand years ago, the Greek spirit emerged. One might speak of the earlier period as the continental era, a term I am happy to use because it expresses the fact that the continental character of this triangular western peninsula is the oldest basic element of its history and prehistory and that our culture, our self-awareness, our personality have come to us from the sea. As long as the sea was not essential to the life of this Asiatic cape, Europe, with its relatively mild climate and favorable natural conditions, was a classic invasion area open to all manner of migrations and expansion movements sweeping in from the east. It remained a classic invasion area for many centuries. But ever since Mediterranean traits became stronger than the original, purely continental ones and the foundations were laid for the fundamental characteristics that would define Europe, there has been a consciousness distinguishing Europe from Asia, the West from the East, and the European from the non-European. At Marathon and Salamis, face to face with Darius and Xerxes, this consciousness received its first brilliant affirmation. A thousand turbulent years later, on the Champs Catalauniques—the battlefields near

3

Orléans and Mauriac—that affirmation was repeated against Attila. Between Tours and Poitiers, where the forces of Islam were rolled back from the Loire, it was affirmed anew in the battle against Abd-el-Rahman and Abd-el-Melek.

Until long after the Renaissance—that is, until comparatively recently—the history of Europe was partly determined by the fact of its being an invasion area. As heirs of Herodotus, we could describe the history of the West in terms of a semipermanent stream of large-scale invasions and attacks from the east on the western borders. It would be a chronicle of a semi-permanent state of siege, of attack and counterattack. It would also be, more incidentally, a chronicle of the attacks made from within the beleaguered western fortress, attacks of a limited and somewhat transitory nature and therefore not of lasting strategic value. The attackers were not defeated once and for all; the siege was not lifted permanently. Enemy activity sometimes slackened or was deflected, but it was never conclusively defeated as long as the West continued to be dominated by a defensive mentality. At the end of a lifelong study of the relations between Europe and Asia, and of the Crusades in particular, René Grousset noted no trait more dominant "than Western society's instinct for self-preservation in the face of the most formidable danger it had ever encountered." A main theme, essential to the history of Europe, was its defense against the recurrent threat of an Asiatic tidal wave that would engulf the entire continent. "This became obvious when the West gave up the attempt."[1] The Turks reached the gates of Vienna in 1529.

Nevertheless, though Greek civilization was molded in a way that contrasted sharply with its ancient Asiatic background, it remained mixed in character—for example geographically, to mention only one illustration. It was born in Asia, in Ionia, as a new and superior expression of the achievements of other, older cultures of the Near East and Egypt. It faced toward the east and spread more in an easterly than a westerly direction.

4

One cannot describe it more suggestively than Dawson: it terminated at Alexandria, Antioch, and Byzantium rather than at the Greek colonies to the west in southern Italy.[2] In spite of Rome's mighty role as intermediary between the civilized Hellenic world and the barbarian peoples of Western Europe, Greek thought reached the Atlantic coast and took glorious possession of the Western spirit via paths far removed from the western route. And so it may be said that although the Greeks shaped the European spirit by opposing Asia, they were nevertheless oriented toward Asia.

Viewed in this way, Hellenism is the logical expression of a paradoxical combination of opposing motives. This paradoxical combination seems to be a second basic theme of Mediterranean civilization. The circumstances and factors of the Roman era were in no way similar, but the Mediterranean dual nature continued to exist in their world, especially after the death of Marcus Aurelius. Here, too, one finds a combination of hostility and inclination, of rejection and reabsorption, in the attitude toward the peoples of the outside world and Asia, particularly where spiritual matters were concerned.

Then, finally, the third theme of the Mediterranean civilization that created Europe appears to possess a corresponding dual nature. Jewish-Christian history is filled with strife and resistance. Its origins, like those of the Greek consciousness in a sense, are rooted in an antithesis to "Asia." But it also contains the precept that man should love his neighbor, even his enemy, as himself. Does this mean that from the time of its inception our culture has known a fundamental ambivalence in its relations with the outside world, as European man has toward non-European man?

A marked dualism does appear to be the first fact to strike an observer of the European's attitude toward the world outside. There seems to be a continuous dual relationship based upon a fundamental theme clearly connected with the Mediterranean past. Two relations, separate but indivisible, are always apparent in the European consciousness. One is in the realm of political life in its broadest sense, in the atmosphere of—if I may describe it so—concrete relations with concrete non-European countries, peoples, and worlds. This is the relationship that freely employs political, military, socioeconomic, and sometimes missionary terminology. It is this relationship that has also, in general, dominated the pens of the historians who have recorded the history of our Western resistance and of our expansion. The other relationship has reigned in the minds of men. Its domain is that of the imagination, of all sorts of images of non-Western people and worlds which have flourished in our culture—images derived not from observation, experience, and perceptible reality but from a psychological urge. That urge creates its own realities which are totally different from the political realities of the first category. But they are in no way subordinate in either strength or clarity since they have always possessed that absolute reality value so characteristic of the rule of the myth. This will receive our full attention in due course.

But I wish to accord precedence to one fact: the problem of this dual relationship is a contemporary one that deeply concerns us Europeans of the twentieth century. We have witnessed historical developments on a worldwide scale; we are the generation for whom this relational problem is of central importance. We were born in an era when Europe still seemed to be—and perhaps was—Queen of the World. Yet the West's great retreat from Asia and Africa, which spelled the visible end of our classic expansion and of Western mastery of the world, has taken place within the space of less than one generation. A complete reversal of the relations between the Western and non-Western worlds has come about in our time. We have witnessed a tremendous event requiring insight, interpretation, and explanation, even though we may, in the meantime, be

6

unable to provide more than a mere provisional explanation of a very general nature. The historians can set about their work later. But if it is characteristic of critical periods of transition that roots are laid bare and exposed to our gaze, then the period in which we live gives us every opportunity to achieve insight or, in any event, spurs us on to make the attempt.

André Siegfried, who first visited India in 1900 in the course of a journey around the world, seems to me to have penetrated to these roots when he revisited that country in 1950. He compared the world he found with the one he had known in 1900. Then the power of Europe had seemed not only to be absolute but to derive from the natural order of things; that same power now seemed to be doomed to extinction, at least in that part of the world. Then the formula *civis europeanus sum* had opened all doors, as the *civis romanus sum* had done in a former age; now many doors were closed to the civis europeanus.

> The European's position in Asia [he wrote] is under attack from the Soviet Union in the name of the revolution and in the name of the various local brands of nationalism; it is under attack from the United States in the name of anticolonialism and, thirdly, from the Asians themselves in the name of their own spiritual superiority. We have responded to these attacks with humility; we have bowed our heads before the often direct accusations and reproaches that Eastern thinkers have leveled at our materialism, our excessive ambition, and our inordinate desire for comfort and wealth. Of course we cannot but concede the justice of such complaints. But the admiration we feel for some sublime Eastern minds should not prevent us from pointing out that social progress is a Western concept. It is by no means certain that our departure will, in fact, bring any improvement in the condi-

7

tion of the masses. Christian charity, Shakespeare's milk of human kindness, seems to be an attribute of Western culture. Asia is not a continent where man feels compassion for his fellow man. I do not believe, therefore, that the humble and apologetic attitude we have too often assumed is justified.[3]

This statement is an extremely lucid and logical exposition of the duality of our attitudes. The Europeans with whom we are concerned and whose being and vocation is, in the well-known phrase of Cecil Rhodes, "to do or to die," appear here in all their ambitious expansionism, with their economic savoir faire, their social ideology, and their organizational talents (which are of such tremendous and decisive practical significance to the whole world). At the same time, the current political and ideological vulnerability of these qualities is crystal clear; the European is shown to possess a psychological disposition out of touch with all political reality. It exists independently of objective facts, which seem to have become irrelevant. It is a disposition that leads him to choose "to die" rather than "to do" and forces him to repent of his wickedness, covetousness, pride, and complacency. This phenomenon led Pieter Geyl to refer to our naïve "illusionism."[4]

Although illusionism may be rejected, it cannot be ignored. The historical significance of this reality is just as far-reaching as that of our expansive energy. We Europeans seem to be suffering from a fundamental inner split. "To do or to die" seems to polarize our innermost beings. Our lives seem to be based on two realities which are equally absolute but not comparable. Both form an integral part of our relation to the surrounding world. Is the paradoxical unity of these two fundamentally different relationships a modern expression of the dual character of our origin? Like two harmonic progressions, the themes are parallel but separate. And although one progression (that of "concrete" politics) deals with such realities

8

as law, agriculture, and government policy, or with markets, education, and raw materials, their significance is highly deceptive from the point of view of the other progression: its real, concrete appearance belies the secondary, shadowy nature of its content. The other progression considers the hard reality on which politics bases its case to be purely illusory; it is altogether surpassed by another, more absolute truth, a sort of revelation, the positive facts of which lie beyond all perceptible reality, thus transcending and rendering relative all simpler positive facts. It is "the only revelation valid for reality."[5] If the one points to history as its justification, to former realities which have produced real situations with their attendant consequences for the future, the other deems this worthy of no more than a smile. It bases its feeling of superior worth on a different past, one far anterior to the history of the historians; it is a mythical past in which the essentials of life preceded what we now call life, history, culture. The primitive fellowship of man, not as yet removed beyond our range of vision by historical error, revealed the true meaning of life for all eternity.

It is an insoluble contrast between two opposite currents. Reality as opposed to myth? An urge toward expansion as opposed to an urge toward regression? Many formulations of this type, which differentiate but do not separate, spring to mind. The two threads are interwoven like warp and woof and cannot be disentangled.[6] They form, in combination, the historical reality in which the myth makes its way through the centuries with some measure of inner reality and the political reality is not lacking in mythical content. If the regressive attitude expressed in the form of humility, modesty, and apology is of a preeminently mythical character, the myth is not absent from the expansive aspect either. Ernest Seillière devoted his life to a study of this subject.[7]

With respect to our humility and the attendant urge toward regression, two elements appear to be of great significance.

The first is the Christian charity of Mediterranean origin which André Siegfried described as an essentially Western trait. In the "positive" list of virtues that our culture tends to distinguish from the "negative" list of sins (the differentiation to which Johan Huizinga attached such crucial importance) charity has long occupied a prominent position as the shining example of virtue. Did not St. Paul say that it was greater than faith itself? This virtue, above all, is responsible for our social ethos; on the other hand, it undoubtedly bears some responsibility for our tendency toward humility and our feelings of guilt.

The second element is our mythical image of the "noble savage": the myth of the natural and fundamental goodness of primitive man. The world of ideas that produced the noble savage is older than Christianity. It bases its claims on a mythical prehistoric past from which it has extracted an image of man in another, remote, and unknown society; his exemption from our heavy burden of ancient culture leaves him untainted and good, as we too are supposed to have been until the dawn of our history, when Western man began his pilgrim's progress through the ages. Long ago, "in the beginning," in that wonderful first chapter of man's existence on earth, there was a golden age that met its end in a terrible catastrophe. This was the beginning of our fall from the heights of original bliss; this was the beginning of our degeneration. Since then we have drifted further and further from our lustrous origins. It is true that Christ's message of reconciliation and redemption holds out a prospect of liberation from this process of degeneration, but the old, never entirely forgotten idea of an ideal age has, through constantly changing interpretations, continued to offer opportunities for culture to make contact with that unfaded prehistory; all idealism, all morality, all unattainable dreams of happiness from humanity's obscure beginnings, which form a vivid contrast with present-day shortcomings, will then shine forth. The "noble savage," unknown to the Book of Genesis, was born in that earthly Paradise and seems

10

to have escaped God's attention when Adam and Eve were driven forth, for he remained when the angels with the flaming swords barred our entrance to the Garden of Eden forevermore.

So the "noble savage," or a tenuous prefiguration of him, has been present in our culture from earliest times, but his existence was in an unimaginably remote past at an immeasurable distance of time. "In the beginning" was the paradisiacal condition of man before the catastrophe brought degeneration and before Cain killed his brother Abel. Paradise: this was an image of a real historical past, even though it might be unimaginably remote. Man once lived in Paradise, in brotherhood, without care, without pain, without suffering, sickness, or death: *in felicitate paradisii*. The great disaster destroyed all this. Although the real nature of the disaster could be interpreted in many ways the question of human guilt was never in any doubt. The fatal calamity may have been caused by the wicked design of the serpent in Paradise or it may have borne a promethean or some other character:[8] human guilt changed everything. Man erred in his use of free will, *a liberi arbitrii malo usu,* and his painful journey began: *series huius calamitatis exorta est* (St. Augustine, *Civitas Dei,* XIII, 14). This was also the Hesiodian view in ancient Greece, while the medieval longing for that lost past never slackened. The belief that our culture is essentially a mistake, wrong, a symptom of degeneration—as stressed by Rousseau—is as old as Latin Christianity, even older: it is as old as our Mediterranean civilization itself. The glorification of all things primitive, the cultureless as a characteristic of the true, the complete, the only and original bliss: that is one of the fundamentals of our Western civilization. It is as fundamental as the disconsolate self-reproach that all this bliss that might have been ours was lost through our own fault, *nostra maxima culpa.* This view of history was not abandoned until the sixteenth century.[9]

There was at first no thought of identifying this mythical

image with any sort of contemporary reality. The myth, the idealization, the identification were for the time being related only to Christianity and to its past. It went no further. The God of the West knew no other worlds or, at any rate, had never made a clear statement regarding any such worlds; and the classical world of antiquity and its geographers were unaware of any world in Africa east of the Indus or beyond the lower reaches of the Nile. No legends relating to India and China, Australia, Oceania, or America had reached the West, while only in the case of Ethiopia had vague rumors of biblical and classical origin penetrated to Europe.[10] Even if only for this reason the myth remained an internal matter: no means of relating it to the contemporary world presented itself. The savages known from experience and from legend were Attila's Huns. They were not "noble," and no thoughts of the blessedness of the primitive state attached to them. In a following stage it was the Saracens, but their claim to any identification with Paradise seemed to be just as slight. The *Song of Roland* exposed the Mussulman in all his heathen wickedness.

The myth could be associated, however, with lands and peoples of less positive reality as, at length, indeed happened. Then the Brahmins or the Camerins, living somewhere to the east near the Indus, became the objects of mythical conjecture. Those who lived there may not have been christened but they were instinctively Christian; if this was not Paradise itself it was certainly very near to it.[11] And although that might not mean a completely paradisiacal existence, it still approached it more closely than the sinful way of life in the Christian West. Opinions on the Scythians varied somewhat but they too were often included in the images of men such as Adam of Bremen, who ventured opinions concerning the existence of the Hyperboreans to the north, a race that also lived in a state of almost original beatitude.

But as long as Latin Christianity remained spiritually and geographically sealed off from the rest of the world it went on

12

relating its images of the primitive age, which were just as real as its own faith, to itself, projecting them all back to "the beginning." But its vision broadened before long to become, at first, Mediterranean again, as Henri Pirenne (although with a completely different end in view) has shown so convincingly. And finally it acquired a Western view of the world. This was to open up undreamed-of possibilities as far as the myth was concerned.

The Crusades, that spectacular chapter in the great confrontation between Europe and the world beyond, undoubtedly fulfilled a central function in this development. Large-scale sorties from the beleaguered Western fortress in the twelfth and thirteenth centuries revealed new horizons and created a new outlook. On the one hand, the attempt to destroy Europe had failed; it had escaped the Mongol and Mohammedan threat. At the same time, enticing perspectives in the East offered themselves for exploration. As we know, Pope Innocent IV despatched Jean du Plan Carpini as his special envoy to the Great Khan in 1245, and before long, in 1253, Willem van Ruusbroec undertook his famous journey to the Khan Monga at the behest of Louis IX of France. Far-reaching possibilities, the consequences of which were incalculable, seemed to be opening up. The voyages and descriptions of the famous travelers and pseudo-travelers of the thirteenth and fourteenth centuries—Marco Polo, Mandeville, and others—now followed. They pioneered new flights of thought, conjuring up images of immense Asiatic riches before the incredulous eyes of the West: Cathay, India, the realm of the Great Mogul. And even though their accounts may not have been observations in the strict sense of the word they created worlds surrounded by a faint aura of mystery, worlds which lent themselves to an endless variety of interpretations and onto which all the old images and ideas could be projected.

India now becomes an important part of our theme. For it was there, in the twelfth century, that the legendary kingdom of Ethiopia (or part of it at any rate) was localized in the shadow of the Caucasus.[12] We cannot doubt that its appeal to the imagination derived first and foremost from biblical and classical legend. The Queen of Sheba, of whom Kings 1:10 tells, was looked upon as an Ethiopian monarch. According to Acts 8:28, the eunuch in charge of the treasure of Queen Candace of Ethiopia was converted to Christianity at Jerusalem, an event that was followed by the christianization of Ethiopia. This old tale, however, now took on a new, concrete meaning. The idea gathered momentum that the old Christian kingdom of Ethiopia might perhaps prove to be an ally on the other side of the hostile world of Islam. For in spite of the many courtesies shown by both sides, and their numerous economic and cultural ties,[13] the fact remained that the two worlds of Christianity and Islam "were each, in their beliefs, definitely closed societies, each a *societas perfecta* which, in religious matters, permitted no compromise."[14] Fundamentally, they were still irreconcilably hostile.

All sorts of detailed accounts of Ethiopia now reached the West and caused hitherto nebulous ideas to take clear and expressive shape, crystallizing Europe's image of Ethiopia in a highly positive way. They revived memories of old legends that suggested the existence of traditional and natural ties between Ethiopian and Latin Christianity. If Islam had severed these ties in the seventh century, by virtue of its geographical position, it now seemed possible to renew the contact in accordance with the real nature of things. The prospect of joint opposition to the world of Islam excited the imagination. Europe now distinctly visualized the rediscovered country as the blessed kingdom of Prester John who ruled, as Priest-King, over a territory known to extend from East Africa to beyond the Indus. To the south it was said to be bounded by the ocean; to the north the Nile connected it with the Mediterranean, while to the west, according to the geographers following in the footsteps of Idrisi (1150), a tributary of the Nile thought to flow

14

westward via Lake Chad linked it with the Atlantic Ocean. This junction with the Atlantic was considered an established fact for all later geographers and cartographers such as d'Ailly, Toscanelli, Behaim, Schöner, Plancius, and Ortelius, and well into the seventeenth century it was still accepted by Blaeu, Dapper, and others.[15] So it was believed, at any rate until the sixteenth century, that contact with this natural ally was the key to the future triumph of Christianity over Islam.[16]

Ethiopia had a powerful hold on the imagination for yet another reason: it was here that the Nile was believed to have its source. And the exegesis of Genesis 2:10–11 established a connection between the Nile and Paradise. So the renewed interest in Ethiopia now created the possibility of locating the geographical whereabouts of Paradise. Although the question of locality had always exercised men's minds, it had not always been possible to make use of geographical data in the search.[17] Legend related that St. Brendan had found Paradise on an island to the southwest. Adam of Bremen, like his predecessors such as Martianus Capella, had supposed it to be situated to the far north.[18] But popular opinion had long held the un-thinking conviction that the site of the biblical Paradise was in the east. The four rivers referred to in Genesis 2:11–15 could only be the Nile and the Indus, the Euphrates and the Tigris.[19] One therefore finds Marco Polo, for instance, displaying intense interest in the question of the source of the Nile. And John Mandeville, whose work was an encyclopedia of the knowledge and beliefs current in his time (1370), stated that although he had not personally visited Paradise and was thus unable to provide much information about it, he could never-theless say that it was situated to the east.[20]

The image thus became a geographical reality. It was re-moved from a distant past to a distant present. Where at first it had been characterized by the distance in time, it now became increasingly invested with a contemporary character. The distance became a matter of geography.[21] Of course this Paradise, the approximate site of which was now thought to be known, was closed to mankind in accordance with Genesis 3:24. But the Christian Ethiopians' physical proximity to it was interpreted as highly significant. They could not be far removed from a true state of bliss, and therefore from every point of view contact with them could only mean an immense gain for Latin Christianity and for the cause of Christianity versus Islam.

The figure of Prester John, the Ethiopian Priest-King, appealed to the imagination of the late Middle Ages. No one knew him, but his person and his realm were described in minute detail by contemporary writers. Their accounts evoked a string of fascinating and fundamental questions, for the image of the Priest-King was closely in tune with the needs of the time.[22] What were felt to be the perils of the situation caused him to be regarded first and foremost as a powerful ally who would deliver the Christian world from the permanent danger of Islam. A much more widely held expectation, in evidence throughout the Middle Ages, was based on an even deeper conviction: the coming of the Emperor-Redeemer, the great Prince of Peace, which would be followed by a conclusive battle between the forces of Light and the forces of the Antichrist resulting in the certain victory of the former. Thus clothed in symbolism, the prophecy had predicted the end of the world at an indeterminate moment, and each successive generation had interpreted this in terms of contemporary persons and problems. Europe now became aware of a connection between this expectation and the almost celestial ruler of blessed Ethiopia. Was he immortal? Even in periods not linked by time it was always the selfsame Prester John who was the subject of speculation. It had been rumored since the twelfth century that John had sent a letter to the Emperor at Constantinople, and for several centuries after Pope Alexander III referred to his "beloved son John the illustrious and glorious king of India" (1170) the miraculous Prince continued to dominate

16

the Western imagination.[23] His envoys were said to have come to Europe in the fourteenth century, visiting Rome, Naples, France, and Aragon. Nevertheless, he was still regarded as a contemporary in the middle of the fifteenth century, and Prince Henry the Navigator, in the last year of his life (1460), intended or at least wished to go to the country of this King of Kings in order to meet him in person.[24] He could not fail to be the object of all sorts of different interpretations, and one of the oldest of them would seem to be particularly relevant at this point. In his famous *Chronicon,* Otto von Freising (1150) established a relationship between the Ethiopian royal family and Caspar who, according to the later Evangelists, was the King of India (which included Ethiopia) and one of the Three Magi who journeyed to Bethlehem.[25]

Meanwhile, the concept of the Three Kings had undergone a lengthy and remarkable development.[26] The vague group comprising an unspecified number of magi referred to in Matthew 2 had, in the course of the centuries, become a colorful and minutely described trio. First their number was fixed at three, and it was not long before they were described as kings. They appeared in a sixth-century Armenian gospel as King Melchior of Persia, King Caspar of India-Ethiopia, and King Balthazar of Arabia. But the *Legenda Aurea* written in the thirteenth century by Jacobus de Voragine showed that another important element had been added: in the combination that was to become Christian tradition the Three Kings also represented three generations, thus symbolizing the whole of humanity.[27] Moreover, racial differences between the monarchs appeared in the thirteenth century and were thenceforward closely related to certain peoples. Although there is no means of verifying it, one wonders whether in the course of the Middle Ages they might not have undergone a certain symbolic identification with the sons of Noah. There is frequent mention of them. Ham, the youngest, is associated with Africa; Shem with the East (Asia); and Japheth with Greece (Europe).[28] The depraved Ham was the mighty Croesus from whom Nimrod was descended. Shem was the progenitor of the Saracens, which was not much better. Japheth was the father of the Israelites and of the Europeans. By the beginning of the fifteenth century Caspar, the youngest of the Three Magi (although by now he had become noble), was also depicted as an "African" in art and literature while Balthazar was a relatively indeterminate Oriental, and Melchior, the oldest, a white European. Two points deserve special attention. One is that the Negro thus appeared "canonized" in our culture before the Indian was discovered. The second is that this racial aspect combined with the older theory of the three generations almost suggests a primitive form of the modern metaphorical reference to "young nations," where colored peoples are meant.

So Prester John came to be seen in many perspectives, being linked with Caspar, with Queen Bilqis of Sheba whose dominions Josephus had localized on the Nile, and with the myths relating to an earthly Paradise. Pierre d'Ailly, whose famous work *Imago Mundi,* written at the beginning of the fifteenth century, contained all the geographical knowledge of his day and had such a profound effect on Columbus, provided a full account of the theories put forward over the years concerning both Ethiopia itself and the nature of its inhabitants. He thus expressed the pronounced interest which the late Middle Ages took in the Ethiopian question.[29] When the Portuguese began their voyages of exploration along the west coast of Africa in the middle of the fifteenth century, one of their principal aims was to find a channel of communication with that mysterious Christian kingdom, either by means of the great river referred to by all geographers or by means of another route along the eastern shore of the Guinea coast which the Genoese Vadino and Guida Vivaldi were said to have followed two centuries before. Vasco da Gama carried letters for Prester John as Columbus was to do later for the Great Khan.[30]

It seems to me an essential part of our theme that the whole

18

of this Ethiopism with its paradisiacal streak, its excessive identification with biblical texts, and its expressive ethnical character derived its particular significance from the bitter struggle between Christianity and Islam. Although the interpretation of all real and imaginary facts was tinged with a strong mythical quality, all this mythomania was nevertheless directed toward a positive political end. Pierre d'Ailly, for instance, never lost sight of one consuming idea: the struggle against Islam and, more especially, the war against the Turks who were pressing in on the southeast. Once they were defeated the whole of the East could be liberated.[31] The events of the following century illustrated his political perspicacity, quite irrespective of the religious enthusiasm upon which it was based. Realistic views such as these spread throughout the West with the fame of *Imago Mundi* even before the book was printed around 1480.[32] It is difficult to assess the extent of d'Ailly's influence, but it is likely that he was of immense significance to the world voyagers of the next period. Political motives achieved such prominence in the course of the fifteenth century that the question which had given rise to Ethiopism— the location of Paradise—could gradually disappear without in any way affecting the intensity of the Western world's expectations.

The question of Paradise did not fade from men's minds, but it progressively ceased to be linked with the legendary Ethiopia. The world now appeared to be so immense, so very much greater than had been supposed; new knowledge required new interpretations. The geographers who came after Pierre d'Ailly sought Paradise more and more to the west, following in the footsteps of St. Brendan, whose history was endowed with greater authenticity. In his third letter Columbus expressed the view that Paradise was situated south of the Equator, lying somewhere on top of a mountain in the land recently discovered.[33] Leo Africanus, the remarkable early sixteenth-century traveler who gave an objective and fairly

19

accurate account of his journey through Africa, describing the countries and peoples he had seen, made no mention of the paradisiacal character of Ethiopia, nor is there any reference in his *Navigazzioni* to a river flowing westward.[34] Belief in a connection between Ethiopia and Sheba lived on, however, and Leo provided particulars—culled from Ethiopian sources —regarding the Ethiopian diplomatic mission to Pope Eugenius IV in 1440. But the picture painted by the *Navigazzioni* was soberly factual, sapping the roots of many a mythical interpretation.

At length John II of Portugal despatched envoys in search of Prester John. Pedro de Covilha and Afonso de Paiva, disguised as merchants and supplied with credentials, money, and goods, left Portugal for East Africa in 1486 or 1487. After many wanderings, de Covilha eventually reached Ethiopia, where he was received with honor. The Ethiopians had developed their own image of the outside world, however, and he was refused permission to leave. According to the reports of later Portuguese travelers he finally resigned himself to his fate, married an Ethiopian wife, and settled down with his family in the land of the King of Kings.[35] In spite of his misfortune, and notwithstanding the modified popular image which no longer centered its dreams of Paradise on the ancient country of Prester John, the orientation toward Ethiopia long remained unchanged, and Latin Christianity acknowledged the *bon éthiopien,* the good Negro on whom all sorts of definite and indefinite expectations continued to be centered. His was to be a strange fate.[36]

Meanwhile another figure, in a sense even more remarkable, had captured the imagination of the West. The longer one thinks of his role the more complicated it becomes. He makes his appearance in the twelfth-century French novel *Floire et Blanceflor,* which ere long was to spread his fame far beyond the borders of France. Without a doubt the novel owed its existence to the direct and powerful influence of the Crusades,

20

which had changed the relations between East and West. Even so, the picture presented by *Floire et Blanceflor* showed as yet no evidence of an adequate inner reorientation of the Christian world (in terms of Grousset's *societas perfecta*) toward the world of Islam, which was the enemy. Since the *Song of Roland* the West had been familiar with only that version of the Orient which, as we saw, depicted Mohammed as a scoundrel and his followers as abominable idolaters given to immoral practices such as polygamy and capable of every sort of satanic wickedness. But *Floire et Blanceflor* applied the theme of the "noble savage" for the first time to the East, to Islam, in a form that was to remain a part of our culture throughout the centuries, revealing its presence time and again through art and literature. Here, in the French novel establishing this tradition, the guilty and deeply ashamed Floire and his Blanceflor confront the infamously deceived Babylonian Emir at whose hands they expect their just punishment. But the Eastern potentate, possessing unlimited means of exacting an exemplary vengeance, is moved by the deceivers' love for each other. Quite unexpectedly he reveals himself as a paragon of magnanimity, mercy, and benevolence—charity—for of course our culture can only describe virtue in its own terms. The merciful Emir proudly takes his place at the head of a long line of Orientals who will adorn the pages of European literature in the following centuries, continuing to give expression to the East's mesmeric effect on the Latin spirit. It is not an East based on calm observation, even though it contains many reminders of the Islam now known to Europe. The newly awakened orientalism projected its fundamental characteristics beyond the limits of observed reality, transforming the benevolent Babylonian into a mythical *bon oriental*.

An ethnic sentiment thus tried to affix itself to the Babylonian as it had done in the case of Ethiopia. Although its choice of object could vary constantly it remained unchanged itself in the centuries that followed. Savage: the Emir was this by definition since he was a Muslim, a non-Christian, irrespective of any finer qualities that might be inherent in his own culture. Noble: he was this as bearer of the noblest qualities defined as virtues by Christianity. Object of the image for which our culture felt a need: was he this, after all, in his capacity of the non-European who was the most obvious choice? True, the West knew him better than the Ethiopian, whom it did not know at all; in spite of everything, contact with him was still direct and comparatively close. But a case could also be made for the reverse: that for this very reason the Muslim was less eligible than the Abyssinian Negro, his rival, to become the noble savage of the myth. Just as our opinion cannot be confirmed, history itself was also swayed by doubt. The race between Negro and Muslim to gain the approbation of the West, a contest that had its origins in the twelfth century, had begun. With fortune favoring now one and now the other throughout the centuries, they pursued their course beyond the limits of perceptible reality.

II

Thus a new mentality and the new techniques it employed[37] rapidly brought about a totally different world from the fifteenth century onward, but this new world and the techniques that made it possible are less important to our theme than the mentality and motives behind them. We are concerned less with the new knowledge of the earth gathered and transmitted by travelers and geographers than with the new wealth of possibilities for interpretation and identification that opened up a splendid future for the old myths. The two fundamental realities, one in the realm of "concrete" politics and the other in the realm of the myth, remained—and remain now—an unresolved paradox. Distinct and unassailable, they stand side by side as two cornerstones in the accounts of the great adventurers and the explanations of the historians and commentators. The Portuguese expeditions to the islands in the southwest, followed by those to Ceuta on the north coast of Africa and to Guinea, and indeed their systematic exploration of the entire African coastline in the fifteenth century are characterized, like the exploits of Columbus and all the great discoverers who came after him, by this same dual motivation.[38]

In his famous reconstruction of Portuguese exploits the Portuguese chronicler Gomes Eannes de Azurara listed the six characteristics that made Henry the Navigator such an outstanding representative of his age and society.[39] They seem to summarize the entire psychology underlying the approach of the West to the non-West in that critical period. There was, in the first place, Prince Henry's ascetic urge to perform great deeds for the glory of God and the Portuguese king, to discover unknown and distant lands whose existence, unvouched for by knowledge or memory, was based solely on such wondrous tales as those of Brendan. Secondly, he wished to know whether these countries were inhabited by Christians with whom it would be safe to trade. Thirdly, the discovery of an African country could mean that it would be possible to obtain a more exact impression of the real extent of the Islamic world—and it was important to know the full strength of the enemy. Fourthly, the West, and of course Portugal in particular, might find a Christian ally willing for love of Jesus to provide effective help in the struggle against the Moors. It was conceivable that a Christian African monarch might be of greater assistance to Portugal in its life and death struggle with the enemy of the faith than Europe had in fact proved to be. And then there was the fifth factor: a profound longing to propagate the faith and to save souls through conversion. Azurara considered the sixth factor, however, to be the weightiest of all. It was not a motive in the usual sense of the word, but a force to which Prince Henry and Portugal and all of us, he said, are subject: the power of the stars. Azurara added that, although as a Catholic he was bound to state first of all that predestination might, with the help of God's grace, be avoided by the use of sober judgment, those who are predestined to greatness are better advised to follow the course marked out for them, thus adding luster to their achievements.

The psychological urge behind the initiative that was to result in the expansion of the West was here put into words. It inspired great deeds directed toward goals on both sides of the borderline between the two indivisible but irreconcilable realities. For in addition to such purely geographical, political, and economic incentives[40] as the African coastline and in-

24

terior, the possibility of forming an alliance with the isolated Christian kingdom assumed to be there and trading with other Christian nations (no one considered the possibility of finding non-Christians), there were also myth-inspired motives such as the conviction of being chosen for the task, the desire (up to a point) to play a missionary role, and a rapidly growing belief in the *bon nègre* who would help for no reason other than true love of Jesus, in contrast to the many Europeans whose aid had been so inadequate. The newly discovered peoples would be notable for their refinement, their nobility, and the purity of their faith; they would be courteous and hospitable and, in short, something like Nicolò de' Conti's portrayal of them earlier in the fifteenth century[41]—a portrayal in which the Mohammedans were treated with respect because, de' Conti said, he had observed how well they measured up to high cultural, moral, and social standards.

As might be expected, these motives recur, *mutatis mutandis,* in the letters and the (disputed) journal of Columbus. Azurara's threesome of missionary, merchant, and soldier once again journeyed across the ocean, this time united in the person of Columbus. Again we find an inextricable interlinking of the two chains of different realities. The opening up of the Western world was, in its design, on the same order as the circumnavigation and exploration of Africa and subsequently of South and Southeast Asia. For that design was squarely based on the view—which Columbus shared with his contemporaries—that although the route might be different the goal was the same. In its main outlines Azurara's portrait of Prince Henry largely corresponds to the figure of Columbus. He too was chosen to serve God and the cause of Christ—his mission having, at the same time, political and economic content. The gold could be used for the reconquest of Jerusalem; trade with the Great Khan, even though he was no Christian, would flourish and yield large profits to Their Majesties the King and Queen of Spain.[42] By and large, that was the view

25

of Alvaro Velho, who sailed with Vasco da Gama in search of the obscure Christian Kingdom—with all the implications of that search—but whose *Roteiro* opened with the words "In the name of God. Amen. In the year 1597 King Emmanuel, the first of this name in Portugal, despatched four ships on a mission of exploration, these ships setting out in search of spices."[43]

But no matter what the priority of motives, they were activated by an irrational psychological urge to make discoveries, to sail beyond the horizon. It was a longing for hitherto unseen places stemming from mythical memory. In October 1492, Columbus was convinced that he had arrived in Old Testament country and was not far distant from the earthly Paradise. Luis de Torres, whom he selected to accompany Rodrigo de Jerez on a reconnaissance mission, was chosen because of his special qualifications for the task. As a converted Jew he knew Hebrew, Arabic, and Chaldaic—the languages that would certainly be required under the circumstances. Did this line of thought hinder a simultaneous, healthy interest in the gold mines? Such abundance was more likely to be attributed to the proximity of Paradise. Moreover, from time immemorial legend had presented the Atlantic as a sea filled with wonders. Wondrous islands supposedly dotted the route to Paradise, which Columbus now thought to be located to the southwest. Once again, it is all consonant with St. Brendan.

And now, at the dawning of the "Atlantic" era, the American Indian was admitted to the ranks of the noble savages. His qualifications for the role of "savage" were determined by circumstance: he was, after all, discovered in a relatively primitive state. It is thought that his endowment with the quality of "noble" may have owed a great deal to Italian influence.[44] Perhaps he was immediately included in the spell cast by the bucolic and Arcadian poetry of the Italian Renaissance that depicted and distorted primitive life after the style of Vergil. The latter indubitably had its effect on Columbus and Vespucci. The dreams of the Arcadian poets corresponded closely to descriptions such as that by Pietro Martyr d'Anghiera, who extolled the heavenly qualities of the New World, investing its inhabitants with all the attributes of purity, brotherly love, and perfection which God had intended for mankind before the Fall.[45] Having made his entry into the Western imagination, the red Indian was before long to occupy a central place there, which he retained, with some fluctuation, until the advent of the Indian novel in the nineteenth century. During this period his features provide the model for the classic type of noble savage. His influence on the European spirit is yet another marked example of the absolute disjunction and indivisible interrelationship of fact and myth.

In actual fact, there were descriptions—by Cortes, Vespucci, Gomara, Herrera, Pietro Martyr, and others—of lands and peoples on the other side of the Atlantic. In actual fact too, there were the ruthless massacres of the Aztecs, the Incas, and other Indian peoples, who were reduced to an estimated 20 per cent or less of their original number. The myth, however, provided the European imagination with a different Indian. He assumed the form outlined for him by the Western spirit long before—perhaps even in as remote a past as the beginning of our civilization: a member of that ideal society whose general characteristics were believed to correspond to certain main features of the paradisiacal condition which had been free of the burden of civilization, knowing neither human wickedness, suffering, nor want. The placid Pietro Martyr depicts the primitive Indian world (though what may, in fact, be termed primitive?) as a sort of last remnant of an *aetas aurea,* a golden age, a Vergilian *saturnium regnum.* The Indians' physical beauty, their fine bodies and noble features, were found to be the logical accompaniment to a noble nature.[46] That nobility, the sole prerogative of primitive peoples, manifested itself as a sort of childish innocence.

Columbus' first letter contains a lyrical account of the child-

27

like goodness of the Indians of La Spañola. Naturally good, peaceable, cordial, and hospitable, their trust is absolute once their initial fears have been dispelled, and they are content with even the most trifling of gifts, he declares. His impression is that want and private property are both unknown. Their society seems to lack any economic system and to be, in a material sense, completely egalitarian in that the communally held possessions are sufficient to satisfy the desires of all. They are small, fraternal, communist societies not unlike Paradise. They shine forth in even greater splendor when compared with some other Caribbean peoples about whom even the Indians of La Spañola tell the most spine-chilling tales. The people of Caniba, for instance, have tails, dog-like heads, and only one eye; they are cannibals who are unbelievably savage in all respects—displaying some similarity with the Cynocephalae of Mandeville's fantasies. Although many people took Sepulveda's side in his dispute with Las Casas and made much of the reports of the supposed cruelty and inferiority of some savages, the dominant sentiment regarding the Indian—the savage *par excellence*—was one of admiration and esteem. The authors of sixteenth- and seventeenth-century utopian literature, to which attention will be devoted later, usually had the Indians in mind as models.

And so all eyes were turned to the west. Campanella based much of his ideal state, the *Civitas solis,* on what he thought he knew of the Incas, whom Pizarro had exterminated. And the same may be said of many imaginative fancies of this type: Godwin's *Man in the Moon,*[47] Cyrano de Bergerac's *Voyage dans la lune* and *Histoire comique des états et empires du soleil.*[48] Montaigne wrote *Livre des Coches*[49] on the basis of information about Brazil derived from Villegagnon.[50] The societies of Peru and Mexico were not in the least primitive, and gave no grounds for comparison with the islands where the first truly primitive Indian tribes had been discovered, but these facts made no impression on solidly entrenched popular

28

belief. The theory of the natural goodness of man, a condition to which primitive man corresponded more closely than others, was advanced by Montaigne with the Indians of South America in mind before its later revival by Rousseau.

We are now confronted with the abstruse problem of why the red Indian was so much more privileged, in the myth at least, than the Negro. Surely the claims of the *bon nègre* were more venerable. Were these claims not based on a tradition dating back to the manger of Bethlehem and on Europe's respect and predilection for the legendary Christian kingdom of Ethiopia? Moreover, the Indians were hardly, if at all, Christian; their Christianity, where it existed at all, was of very recent origin. And yet the Indian, with no letters patent of nobility on which to base his appeal, takes the lead from the moment he arrives on the scene. In spite of what fate has in store for him and in spite of the Negro's ancient claims, the Indian never relinquishes this lead except temporarily, as in the eighteenth century when Bougainville, his hopes of Para- guay not fulfilled, found his earthly Paradise in Tahiti, and a short-lived South Seas cult took Europe by storm.[51] This fundamental problem remains unsolved.

For centuries the Negro had existed as a commercial and social reality side by side with his mythical counterpart in the European imagination. Throughout the fifteenth century Negro slavery flourished in Portugal. Did this affect Negroes "from Portuguese soil" who had been slaves of the Moors? In any case the African Negroes whom Antam Gonçalvo brought back to Portugal from his expedition to Guinea after 1443 were a new and stimulating element in the process. On this point Azurara's chronicle of the expedition[52] provides us with highly interesting information, such as the market value of African Negroes (who, when they were not captured directly, could be obtained in exchange for Moorish prisoners of war). We learn from him too that the Portuguese were quick to realize the lucrative character of the new trade. Fact and myth did not clash even then. Although the bodies of the Negroes might be held captive, this very fact made it possible for their souls to achieve true freedom through conversion to Christianity.[53] And so the enslavement of Negroes took on a kind of missionary aspect. It was in keeping that christened Negro slaves should enjoy certain small privileges above their fellows. When, before long, the transport of Negroes to America became the vogue (after 1502 according to some authorities, before 1500 in the opinion of others such as Herrera) those who had been christened were exempt—at least in theory. The idea of transporting them did not originate with Las Casas; when he expressed his views on the subject in 1517 the practice had already been established for something like twenty years. What Las Casas did, which earned him both fame and hatred, was to protect the Indians from the harsh practices of the Spaniards; it was he who pointed out the Negro's superior physical capacity for heavy labor.

The enslavement of unchristian Negroes, whose paganism the sixteenth century vehemently condemned, spared the Indians, believed to be amenable to conversion.[54] The argument was that slavery was rampant in Africa itself, which was therefore anything but a primitive Paradise.[55] It followed that enslavement meant no more to the Negro than a change of owner. Although slavery was in fact common in Indian societies (the Cumana Indians, for instance), Las Casas defended it on the ground that it was a form of domestic service rather than slavery in the European sense of the word; the Indian slaves were more like members of the family. A more practical motive for enslaving the Negro was also evident: the Negro's working capacity was four times that of the Indian's. Finally, there was an aesthetic motive. The contrast between black and white, dark and light, is deeply rooted in us[56] as representing in all respects the ethical contrast between sin and virtue. In describing the first Indians he saw, Columbus, like his successors, remarked on their physical beauty: they were not black.

30

Yet unpredictable cultural fluctuations affecting even the aesthetic appreciation of him were still in store for the Negro. He rocketed into favor once more in the eighteenth century. The fact that the word Indian has acquired a capital letter in many European languages, while the word Negro has not, brings us no nearer to a solution of the fundamental problem of why he is so much more privileged than the Negro. The savages known and referred to throughout the following centuries were either Indians or peoples whom the popular image forced into the Indian mold—or what this was taken to be.

Hardheaded practices versus the noblest of humanitarian theories: idealism at variance with realism—a conflict that seems to be expressed in the renowned controversy between Las Casas and Sepulveda. Sepulveda and his followers maintained that the Indians were idolaters, immoral and servile creatures born to be slaves; furthermore, realistic views and methods were called for in the interests of Spain. In opposition, Las Casas and his supporters insisted that the natural goodness of the Indians was of such a high order that they had only to be converted to the true faith to become the most blessed of mortals.[57] If this controversy was characteristic of the century in which it raged it was also characteristic in a broad sense of the whole "Atlantic" era that began when the great discoveries brought the Mediterranean era to a close. In contrast to the European disapproval of the moral standards of primitive societies and the view that the consequent inferiority of such societies should not be without its consequences, the views held by Las Casas and by later figures such as Vitoria, Crucé, and a long line of philosophers in all parts of Europe survived through the centuries. Ideologists and utopians continue the tradition by tending to regard the other way of life— its social and material beliefs and institutions and the moral structure on which it is based—as infinitely superior to our own. This view, the antithesis of the claim of European superiority with all its connotations, furnishes the American Indian

with a climate favorable to his development as a physical incarnation of probity, beauty, and wisdom worthy of our affec-
tion and respect. As we have seen, this idea had also existed
in the Mediterranean era, but then it concerned dream peoples
and figures. And although it is true that it also represented a
reality for Europe, it was a mythical reality. The Emir and his
friendly harem-keeper in *Floire et Blanceflor* were not representative of the real Islamic world. The Atlantic age was the
first to apply the old antithesis to a political reality. Was the
noble savage, in Cocchiara's aphorism, invented (by the eighteenth-century philosophers) before he was discovered?[58] It
is nearer the truth to say that he progressed from a classical,
fixed quantity in the Middle Ages to the point where, in the
sixteenth century, he moved into politics, there to establish
himself in a virtually unassailable position.

Meanwhile the medieval pattern of thought, which had done
without any concrete identification, still persisted in our culture. It added another chapter of its own. It had experienced
primitivism first as a projection in time and then as a projection in space. Both these older conceptions, which had originally been mutually antagonistic, now merged to form a new
shoot strong enough to flourish alongside those already in
existence. Its principal form, Utopia, was to become a favorite
of the sixteenth and seventeenth centuries and to remain so
thereafter, even when its period of literary supremacy was
ended. It expressed a never-slackening desire for a better life,
for a happier human condition and a more righteous society.
And although the idea of Utopia was sometimes couched in
skeptical terms it was nevertheless serious in its search for an
earthly Paradise far removed from the imperfections of our
civilization. It was criticism of our society in particular and
of our culture in general.
On the whole, the ideal states thus depicted were definitely

located to the west, in distant seas,[59] as illustrated by Harrington's *Oceana,* More's *Utopia,* Bacon's *New Atlantis,* and a host of similar works. Blazing a trail for Shakespeare's Prospero, Pantagruel journeyed westward to the Oracle of Bacbuc and finally, like Jacques Cartier, reached Canada. This he did under the direct influence of Thomas More, just as Rabelais was also influenced by More in his conception of the country over which Gargantua reigned.[60] In all probability the oft-mentioned island of St. Brendan to the southwest continued to function as a kind of orientation point. In any case it was still to be found on the maps, lying south of Madeira and the Canary Islands, halfway to Cipangu (Japan), reports of which had reached Marco Polo and which was reputedly an island kingdom east of the Cathay (China) coast. This was the position given by Toscanelli in 1480, for instance, and by Cabot a half-century later. Thule to the north—according to classical legend the most distant of all inhabited countries—also gave rise to speculation. Once Utopia and El Dorado[61] were linked with all these old geographical notions Thule, Brendan's island, the Fortunate Isles, or some other island became the last refuge of all original happiness, wisdom, and nobility—Don Quixote's Barataria.

Europe now acquired an image of a mythical people, primitive children of nature inhabiting a heaven-like country beyond the seas. And while numerous utopias were peopled with noble savages whose features were modeled on the pattern provided by the American Indian, a connecting link grew between Utopia and interpretative observation. It caused the tenuous *aetas aurea,* the original Golden Age that no amount of cultural progress had ever succeeded in eradicating from human memory, to change from a mythical, nebulous dream to a distinct, detailed image of the ideal society. For this reason, it was not long before the search for the authentic Paradise was abandoned. Pantagruel's journey is altogether different from that of St. Brendan a millennium before. But the newly introduced ideal state was certainly no less significant for Western culture than the earlier direct image of Paradise.

The innumerable utopias and wondrous travelers' tales of the sixteenth and seventeenth centuries and later were remarkably consistent in their imagery. Belief in ideal societies where man's original state of bliss is still to all intents and purposes a social reality always involves a small number of recurrent themes which are central to the argument and include criticism of one's own situation. They are, of course, closely related to the ancient theme of a Golden Age, which so many travelers had longed to find in some part of the world. Their feeling that they had been transported back to the Golden Age, "the beginning," through the utopian, exotic delights of first the Antilles, then the American continent, and finally the Pacific Islands (Bougainville) was due in part to the contrast between these new delights and their native countries, which colored and distorted all observation from the outset. Again and again the shortcomings of their own Western way of life shaped their outlook. The comparative principle formed the basis both of accounts of Utopia and of travelers' tales.

At the same time, even though Utopia (which was unrelated to any reality) and primitivism (which was related to the distant lands recently discovered) greatly nourished and stimulated each other, we cannot fail to note a fundamental difference. The nostalgia that gripped the world travelers was a disconsolate awareness of an unattainable ideal lost forever. The utopian image, in contrast, encouraged thoughts of an ideal society that might be ours if only we could manage to fulfil certain requirements. Where primitivism thought on the whole in terms of "no longer," utopianism was mainly concerned with "not yet"; if primitivism mourned the past, utopianism looked toward the future.

Despite their deep interaction, therefore, the two categories are still essentially different. They diverge continually only to reunite once more. The "no longer" category is to remain inexorably tied to the degenerative view of history which holds that time has brought us further and further from our real destiny: happiness. The "not yet" category is shortly to provide the elements comprising the evolutionary view of history which holds that it is possible for man (meaning Western man in the first place of course) to progress by stages to a higher level of happiness. For although our original happiness may have been lost, we are not obliged to submit to fate. This train of thought is almost Augustinian: the phrase *ubi non est necesse ut remaneamus* is found in *Civitas Dei,* XV, 1, which goes at length into the entire question of the Fall and fratricide.

The new exotic language was nevertheless the one used by both views for a considerable length of time. It formed a continual reminder for Europe that only twenty days' journey hence people actually lived without benefit of kings, religion, laws, or social organization and were happy in spite of, or perhaps because of, this fact. In the wake of the *De Orbe Novo* of Pietro Martyr, the breviary for all who were engrossed by the new discovery of the world, discoverers swarmed out of the old world in the sixteenth, seventeenth, and eighteenth centuries in search of new worlds. From Jean de Léry[62] to Chateaubriand they projected their ideals of a lost, primitive state of happiness onto these worlds. Still others who remained at home constructed purely imaginary societies after the example of More's *Utopia,* projecting onto them similar ideals which we could attain *if . . .*

From every conceivable individual and social point of view the virtue of simplicity was always the preeminent cause of the fascination and charm which the savages (of both types of society) continued to hold for the Europeans, whom Valéry might have called *terribles simplificateurs.* It was a simplicity as far removed from the complexities of European life as these peoples, whether real or imaginary, were beyond the geographical horizon of Europe.[63] Even later, when geographers' and ethnographers' accounts had become less highly colored and credulous, the popular belief that simplicity was in every way the basic characteristic of the distant, unknown peoples remained unchanged.[64] At the *individual* level it was expressed by their nakedness, which could be interpreted as illustrative of their uncomplicated moral purity, and by their candor, their natural friendliness, and their gentleness. It found *social* expression in their community life based on equality and fraternity which was thrown more sharply into relief by comparison with other peoples, "wicked savages" (*mauvais sauvages*) whose way of life formed a sorry contrast to this ideal state of affairs, irrespective of whether or not their detractors had first-hand knowledge of them. *Economically,* the distant primitive worlds represented that time of perfect happiness when everything was automatically ours and when all our needs were filled in some magical way without our having to make the slightest effort. Even Columbus, as we saw, remarked on the absence of private property, or at least surmised that it did not exist. Since then the European image of the ideal state, whether primitive or not, has been one of a propertyless and communal society. All this made a deep impression on the Jesuits who, in the century between Père Lejeune and Père Lafitau, developed a predilection for exotic peoples that influenced Europe more profoundly than all other sources combined.[65] Their special talent for establishing contact with these other worlds, their resourceful and independent missionary initiative, and their enthusiasm for work, which seemed to be crowned with success, meant that they were both excellent ambassadors for Europe abroad and excellent advocates in Europe of the non-European peoples—until the Church took an opposing official view.

In 1724 Père Lafitau, in *Moeurs des sauvages amériquains comparés aux moeurs des premiers temps,* explicitly traced a connection between the savages of his time and the early days of mankind when all were equal and everything was shared.

So the Romantics found their "back to nature" ready to hand. Back to man's beginnings—but which beginnings? For the comparisons made by men such as Lafitau were not based solely on the Bible; Vergil, too, was always present in the spirit of the Jesuits. Comparison with the ancients, the Greeks in particular, occurs repeatedly. The *reducciones,* the famous small theocratic societies the Jesuits founded in Paraguay, were perhaps a realization of classical rather than Christian ideals. And although at first, as was natural, their predilection for non-European peoples did not preclude their regarding the nonchristianity of those peoples as essentially a vice (even though all discoverers of the first period strongly emphasized the American Indians' fitness and readiness to be converted), this attitude underwent a gradual change. Was it not written that God had other unchristian flocks as well? *Alias oves habeo qui non sunt ex hoc ovili* (John 10:16). Did this not imply a need for drastic revision? When, under rationalist influence, exoticism attains the status of a full-fledged philosophy in the eighteenth century, its fundamental paganism is the precise quality that is held up as its virtue *par excellence:* even Chateaubriand is to respect the *philosophes nus.*

Exoticism in its eighteenth-century garb was, as we know, destined for a brilliant career. It offered an ideal modus vivendi for the contrasting elements in the degenerative "no longer" and the evolutionist "not yet." When Rousseau, harking back to Montaigne, unfurls the banner of the back-to-nature movement, the contrasting elements are linked up and their fundamental differences are resolved in philosophical harmony. All that was ours in the ideal past at the beginning of man's existence on earth can be regained if only we realize that we lost it through our erroneous choice, our faulty objectives. All reference to a supreme catastrophe has vanished from this new philosophy.[66] A typical feature of almost all eighteenth-century historical and social thought is the central position occupied by conscious human action and a refusal to accept either certain types of myth regarding catastrophes or any suggestion that man is subject to historical laws.[67] It was felt that an unbroken series of erroneous decisions had led to our downfall. But it was also felt that greater insight—rather than Christian promises of grace and salvation—offered man his chance of progress. That view bore no relation to the classical cyclical theory, revived by Giambattista Vico in the eighteenth century, which represented history as a perpetual process in which cultures are born, grow, decay, and die like man himself. A compelling cycle, it was beyond all human agency or influence. The crux of the matter for Rousseau and for the new era was that the desirable possibility of "return," or in any case of a fresh start, was now freely available to us; that, paradoxically enough, it implied an evolution, an ascent to a higher level of happiness; and that the final outcome was entirely up to man himself.

It is well known that the eighteenth century felt a deep affinity for the primitive, whether in a utopian form or not. But how are we to account for the fact that it was in this particular century that the old degenerative myths were able to effect a successful merger with their opposite, the evolutionary view? And why is it that this disorderly amalgam of ideas was able to take possession of the European spirit? Should one seek the answer in the playful character of this century of "regression from profundity and gravity," in Huizinga's words? This was the line taken by Hazard, whose masterwork, *Crise de la conscience européenne,* traced such a connection, pointing out that the eighteenth century was one of those centuries that wished to escape from itself and from the heavy burden imposed by a thousand years of culture, being prepared to make use of any pleasant and interesting means of doing so that came to hand. This desire, which expressed itself in a playful urge for feigned simplicity and simplification, was in harmony with the divergent elements of the newly combined worlds of ideas. A

38

culture wishing to be free of itself, said Huizinga, experiences a perpetual longing for the uncivilized.

But how does one set about simplifying? And how does one find the road back? The problem of whether our civilization was heading in the right direction was a subject of debate throughout the century. Speculation like this is, of course, a common phenomenon that may be found in almost any period. But the practice of making comparisons with non-Western peoples did not play a major role until the advent of the eighteenth century. Europe was adjudged inferior to the non-Western world, which emerged from the comparison as Paradise on earth. Voltaire might not take it too seriously, satirizing all that primitivism and all those dreams in popular verse;[68] even Bernardin de St.-Pierre might oppose too much illusion;[69] but none of this prevented glorification of the savages on the ground of their supposed primitivism.

Now, however, it is above all their *reason* that attracts attention. La Hontan's Adario is the first famous *sauvage de bon sens*.[70] The savage has already drawn level with the European on this score by 1703 and in some ways has even surpassed him. Before long reason is to become one of the principal accouterments of the savages who come to populate European literature. The rational Oriental provides a special eighteenth-century variation on Locke's theme of the natural goodness of man. But the words have now been invested with a different meaning. His rational qualities are not Cartesian but general humanitarian goodness; his primitiveness no longer spells lack of culture; and his goodness begins to drift away from Lafitau's *moeurs des premiers temps*. In order to achieve this, however, European self-criticism had to rise to sensational heights, which it did in every possible form in which criticism might be expressed. Criticism might take the form of discourses on reform, such as were delivered by the famous philosophers, or it might be expressed in more imaginative ways like the prevalent one of painting terrifying pictures of the future likely to befall us as the result of our failure. Or the prospect of realizing a desirable ideal might, in utopian fashion, be represented as subject to the fulfilment of all kinds of conditions.[71] To be sure, these gloomy, admonitory voices were not the only ones to be heard: renowned men such as Condorcet shared Fontenelle's belief in the growth and progress of European civilization.[72] But was the true contrast really between one voice and another? Was our perfectibility not just as much an article of faith on both sides? The question was rather the channels into which that perfectibility should be guided.

In 1750 the young, pious Turgot defined the underlying principle of the problem in his famous *Discours en Sorbonne,* drawing a comparison between Europe and the outside world that was distinguished by the admirable balance it achieved. We should begin, he stated, by recognizing Christianity's absolute superiority to any religion and any form of idolatry the world has ever known. For this reason it would be a grave error to lose sight of the unparalleled blessings—in addition, it is true, to much suffering—which Western Christianity has brought to non-Western peoples and to the red Indians in particular. Baptizing as we go, we have transformed these primitive peoples from savages into human beings, and from human beings into Christians. Where such conversion has taken place, encouraging diligence among the uncivilized and bringing order to their societies—blessings which only Christianity can bestow—and where our vices were not also part of the gift, true happiness has followed.[73] A conjunction of Christianity with *égalité, liberté, vertu et simplicité des moeurs* constitutes true happiness. Turgot was often to return to this analysis in his later works, placing an increasing amount of emphasis on criticism of Western society that bore an unmistakable resemblance to Rousseau's, despite their many fundamental differences. Belief in perfectibility, in the world beyond Europe as well as at home, in man's capacity to pro-

40

gress to a higher level of happiness wherever Christianity has paved the way, once a number of social conditions have been complied with: this was his view in 1750. It was to remain unchanged throughout his career.[74] There is no cheap enthusiasm here, no rash rejection of his own culture. Instead, this is the prelude to a serious attempt to place the whole complex of problems relating to culture, cultural comparison, and evolution on a scientific level. The success of his undertaking will enable Turgot to evaluate the many economic and social consequences of these problems.[75] The special significance of the famous competition sponsored by the Académie of Dyon, in which Rousseau entered, is that it was an official, even an academic enquiry into the state of civilization. Even had Rousseau's answer been different, the question itself would still remain both remarkable and characteristic. It might even be termed representative of the century.

Meanwhile, literature abounds with voyages, memoirs both real and fictitious, and dialogues on the subject which throw the preceding centuries completely into the shade. In the resultant image *Robinson Crusoe*—the book so beloved of Rousseau's Émile—occupies a unique place; that is, the official Crusoe, Defoe's Crusoe, as well as the innumerable imitation Crusoes of the time. For they are indeed innumerable.[76] A few remarks about the most famous Crusoe only. Is Defoe's book really the epic of primitive life that people chose to see in it? Or is it a book celebrating the heroic exploits of the *homo faber europeanus?* It is open to an infinite variety of interpretations, a fact which probably accounts for its long and flourishing existence. *Homo faber* is indeed present as a shining example of his inventive civilization. Facing him are two types of savages: Friday, still on the lowest rung (the evolutionistic connotations are plain) and the hordes of *mauvais sauvages* who wish to kill Friday. This depiction of the noble savage—who is not a Negro—presenting a contrast to the immorality and cruelty prevailing in his surroundings is an

41

exceptional case. There is no question here of a savage who is fundamentally good; nor is there any question of glorifying savagedom. The worldly wise Englishman had a firmer grasp of reality. Should we in our more scientific climate then regard the book as an exposition of a theory of three different stages of man's historical development?[77] Should we subscribe to the nineteenth-century evolutionist view that it is a prehistoric novel in which first the tribe, then Friday (the individual who rises above the crowd), and finally Crusoe himself denote three stages in the origin and growth of civilization?[78] Defoe was not chronologically the first among equals, but rather the first in stature, in versatility, and in multi-interpretability. None of the various Crusoes, who are interesting to compare and highly divergent in purport and design, measures up to Defoe's creation. No one explored the exotic problem and the comparison between culture and primitivism with such profundity or placed them in such perspective as he.

It was not only Crusoe who had imitators: Gulliver had his as well. The embittered Swift unfavorably compared the English (and Europeans in general) with the people among whom Gulliver's travels took him. They are admittedly not authentic savages, but they are sometimes animals (the noble Houynhms) in comparison with whom the stupid and servile Yahoos seem to be human. Although it cannot be said to be an exotic novel it is nevertheless of considerable interest in this context since the form in which it is presented is not only an indictment of society but a characteristic one. Even if we attribute the unfavorable picture Swift presents to his personal disillusionment rather than to general cultural-historical causes, the form in which he gives vent to his disillusionment provides a vivid example of the comparative thought of his day.

The sentiments of the eighteenth century sometimes seemed to have arrived at a crossroads. Two paths beckoned, and it followed and explored both. Along one route comparisons were carried to their ultimate conclusion, causing the outside world to rise steadily in Western regard. Although the procedure followed traditional lines, it arrived at a higher stage of development than ever before. There seemed to be no question of comparison on the second route but rather the absolute superiority of the non-European. Unperceived, the two paths intersected somewhere, but not before there had taken place a curious inarticulate glorification of the whole of savagedom and of other worlds, including those of a high cultural order. The good savage was regarded not so much as a wholly "noble" creature consonant with Old Testament definitions of primitivism or with Christian definitions of morality, nor was he even faintly regarded as "better" as in the comparative approach; he became instead the absolute criterion, a perfect example to be emulated. Nothing about him had to be interpreted as superior virtues in the Western sense. If he was not primitive then he was declared to be so, for words are the obedient servants of all doctrine. If he was perhaps ugly by Western standards he was thereafter beautiful by definition, just as his way of life thereafter became virtue by definition. This would seem to be the only possible explanation for the wave of enthusiasm for China and other lands that swept across Europe and for the uncritical imitation to which it gave rise. Is this exotic relationship solely attributable to sheer playfulness and coquetry? Or do the reasons lie at a deeper level, in what was essentially dechristianization?

For a time the stage is completely dominated by the Chinese, who honor everything: their parents and their ancestors, Confucius—the philosopher who was not a religious founder—and a great deal more. That indicated a different scheme of things, another way of thought. The Jesuits, who introduced them to Europe, were so vastly impressed by them that they were in danger of losing sight of their own missionary purpose. Fired with zeal and admiration, they informed the West of this extraordinary, distant country and built up an image of an East perfect in every way.[79] Once again, they found themselves at variance with the official attitude of the Church, and the Sorbonne added its voice to that of Rome in its condemnation of them. But the new image fitted into the general framework of exotic needs too well, and it could not fail to gain some hold on the European spirit. The brilliant description given by Fernao Mendes Pinto in 1614 had been premature in this respect; the seventeenth century was still too entrenched in its comparative principle.[80] Then the Chinese had functioned as scapegoats: queer yellow people with slanting eyes who were intent on defrauding others under a cloak of the greatest courtesy, an odd downward movement since the centuries when Marco Polo's Cathay was held in high esteem. But now China was seen through the eyes of the Jesuits as an immense, remarkable land of perfect peace. Before long their irreligiousness was to rank in Europe as the Chinese virtue *par excellence*. Consciously and positively atheist, the only nobility they acknowledge are their men of letters, and it was on this account that Voltaire paid tribute to them as intellectuals in every sense of the word.[81] The Far East became the source of inspiration for an almost purely "foreignist" sentiment that was also to include the Siamese for a short time. This sentiment found its fullest expression at the aesthetic level—in interior decorating and gardening, in fashion, decoration, and other elements of style. For after all, the Chinese style was by definition synonymous with perfect beauty.

For that matter, beauty and virtue are to be found together during the whole of the Romantic movement, which eventually produced the adversaries of their close alliance. Quasimodo, the bell-ringer of Notre Dame, is hideous, but to Victor Hugo he is also a symbol of the virtue of compassion. That is to become another favorite theme. But first the exoticism of the eighteenth century extends its aesthetic appreciation to practically all non-Western peoples; it is no longer solely restricted to the American Indians. Shakespeare's Caliban may have

44

been ugly, but then he had not been intended to serve as an example of virtue. The Negro was now the first to be endowed with a certain ornamental significance, thereby showing that he was, after all, able to recover some of the ground unexpectedly lost to the Indian. The numerous *Sociétés des amis des noirs,* which were to exercise such influence on French exotic thought in general and on European thought on the subject of the abolition of slavery in particular, hove clearly into view with the splendidly carved ebony Negroes that decorated the salons of the eighteenth century. Before long a colorful procession of picturesque porcelain figures from widely scattered parts of the world was to follow them to their new destination. Turks, Persians, and other non-Westerners were installed alongside the Chinese; their furnishings gave rise to new styles such as the divan, the ottoman, and the sofa; and the Oriental gained entry to the world of fashion with the turban, a quasi-Turkish style of dress, and all sorts of exotic touches. Strangely enough, the red Indians were not represented. On the other hand, James Fenimore Cooper conceived the idea of the legendary Indian whose celebrated type—slim and athletic, of Grecian proportions, eagle-eyed and hawk-nosed—is still in existence at the present day though it scarcely corresponds to any sort of reality.

But the comparative principle still controlled the main route to the future. And strangely enough the Negro was again its first victim. When Terrasson (1725) introduced his Egyptian, the Philosopher Séthos, into literature for an expressly comparative purpose, he threw his highly civilized qualities into greater relief by placing him against a background of barbarian Ethiopians. That reshuffle was curious for two reasons. In the first place, the Ethiopians were the very people who traditionally had been ranked as noble and devoted to Christianity. In the second place, the *un*civilized were suddenly to be rejected and despised. The exotic sentiment seemed to change course, preferring civilization to primitivism. Nevertheless, primitivism still had a place in Terrasson's scheme of things. For it was simplicity, once again, that Séthos held up to our gaze. The Egyptian philosopher, whose influence was as widespread as that of Fénelon's Télémaque throughout the rest of the century (and in the nineteenth, when Stendhal and the Freemasons admired and praised the book), thus gave an unexpected twist to primitivism. Although it did not sever its ties with exoticism, it shook itself free of the old-style admiration for "the savages." No trace remained of the traditional oneness with nature displayed by authentic savages; the new primitivism advocated philosophical independence of the all-too-worldly and the all-too-material. That is where Séthos excelled, and in his capacity as a philosopher, not as a Christian but as a servant of the Elysian Mysteries, the West placed him far above the European both intellectually and morally. Before long many mysterious Egyptians appeared in the works of poets and musicians. Mozart, in whom so many strands converged, springs to mind here. He was a Freemason and, like the lodges, his attention was caught by the new exoticism. The name of the lodge to which both he and Schikaneder, who wrote the libretto for *Die Zauberflöte,* belonged is characteristic enough: "The Crowned Hope of the Orient." They were all inspired by the new interpretations of the Middle East, by tales of wonders and the images to which they gave rise. Wieland, Müller, and Gebler, and many others, were similarly influenced. The new exoticism, which may be described as a form of introspection, provided a new metaphorical interpretation of primitivism. In *Die Zauberflöte* it is personified in Sarastro, a "man who loves his fellowmen." Papageno is his antithesis, typifying primitivism in the traditional sense, now regarded with amused condescension.

Insofar as Monostatos in *Die Zauberflöte*—"the Moor [whose] soul [is] as black as his face" (as black as Othello, the Moor of Venice)—may be associated with black Africa, he is yet another instance of the special problem the Negro continues to pose. On the one hand, as we saw, he had just regained some ground. On the other hand, he becomes involved at this very moment in a new contrast in which he cannot hold his own. It is the classical contrast with Islam, now placed in a completely new light. Unlucky Negro: our culture had always presented him in unequivocal opposition to the Muslim. But now, quite suddenly, Islam is found to merit admiration. Rapidly and unexpectedly, its star moves into a new orbit and the traditional contrast between Negro and Muslim is reversed. For a century or more Islam, and not the Negro, has been the subject of scientific interest. Oriental studies now contribute to the new movement, giving support to the new admiration of Islam as a noble, fine, and logical religion—the latter quality having a strong appeal.

Simon Ockley, the Cambridge orientalist, now becomes the first specialist to challenge the validity of the thesis that the West is superior to the East.[82] A new reputation for the unfortunate Negro has its origins here, and he approaches the next two centuries as typifying the lowest stage of human development. He is reputed to be an altogether inferior creature, a slave by nature, lacking all historical background—a conception that is to take on an almost absolute value. The distinguished American scholar Melville Herskovits refers to it as the myth of the Negro past.

A combination of circumstances: the late seventeenth-century European travelers in the Islamic world introduce the Muslim into the world of European letters not as a barbarian but as a representative of another, authentic world;[83] Jean Chardin, a Protestant exiled since the revocation of the Edict of Nantes in 1685, travels—not without bitterness at his own lot—in Persia and the Middle East, and the reports he sends back to Europe describe the Persian as remarkable, interesting, and in many ways superior to the Westerner; then Boulainvilliers' *Life of Mohamet,* Galland's translation of *The Arabian Nights,* Savary's new translation of the Koran and, above all, innumerable accounts of journeys, as always both authentic and fictitious, strengthen the position of the Muslim at the beginning of the century.[84] Continually in evidence as an object of comparison, he retains his position up to the end of the century. His influence did gradually subside, the process being hastened by the figure of the Greek looming up beside him— the Greek who was both European and opposed to Islam and Asia. Islam's highest point in European comparative thought was thus reached not at the end but before the middle of the eighteenth century. But even after, in Schiller's words, "the Moor has done his work"[85]—he is no longer a Negro, but a Moor—and is free to depart, he still does not withdraw altogether. His hold on the Western mind is to be prolonged into the Romantic movement of the nineteenth century and beyond.

In spite of the fact that the Turkish legions had reached Vienna, the heart of Europe, in 1683, Islam paved Asia's way to the West. Despite his many bizarre customs, his superstitions, and his sexual excesses, the Oriental came to be regarded as a preeminently sympathetic person. He was regarded, in fact, as an especially interesting figure, since the improper held an inordinate fascination for the eighteenth century. Indeed, sexual licentiousness must have been a factor of extraordinary significance in the whole complex of exoticism and primitivism. One is inclined to believe, in the spirit of Van den Berg's *Metabletica*,[85a] that the exotic nakedness and sexual freedom reported by so many travelers must from the outset have fascinated a Christian Europe hemmed in by so many strict moral rules. Historians have probably erred in neglecting this aspect. But Chardin not only describes the Persian as amorous; he is also a *bel homme, plein d'esprit, d'imagination, d'intelligence; galant, gentil, poli, bien élévé.*[86] He is both sociable and tolerant. Boulainvilliers' admiration exceeded all bounds.

Nevertheless, it was a remarkable change when the interest long concentrated on the Far West (the New World) switched

48

to the East. Although the East had at one time been thought identical with the West—the narrow Atlantic Ocean would, it had been hoped, provide an easier route to Cathay—theory and practice lost contact with each other almost immediately. For the western route came to an abrupt halt at the America of the Indians, while thoughts of the East went no further than Greece and Rome. Martino cites Montaigne as a striking example.[87] He in whom all the threads of his time converged had not been in the least fascinated by the East. In only a few isolated instances did a lost Turk drift into his field of vision or was the prophet Mohammed mentioned. Brazil was the focus of attention. Montaigne need not necessarily have written about a *bon Oriental;* a *mauvais Oriental* would have done as well. His total lack of interest was very strange. The Turks had just ravaged the plains of Hungary; Hungarian popular literature was filled with passionate legends about heroic resistance and the inordinate cruelty of the conquerors. And Vienna was besieged in 1529. Following in this tradition, however, Bossuet also made no reference to an East of any historical significance in his *Discours sur l'Histoire Universelle.*

The shift of interest in the eighteenth century, no matter how clearly it may be reflected in literature and in other ways, was slow to gain access to the popular imagination. East and West still had no separate identity. Despite both the influence of the oriental sciences and the unambiguousness of oriental literature, the *Indes Galantes* (1735) gaily jumbled up Turks, Persians, Hurons, Hindus, and South Sea Islanders into one colorful mass. The principle of contrast dwarfed everything else. Where the sole object was to contrast the outside world with Europe there was no need to differentiate between the various elements of that outside world. It thus lent itself to the mythical-primitivist interpretations which the Europeans needed and to the widely diffuse comparative purposes which they had in view. A psychological urge gave rise to a xenophilia of an entirely general nature.

The Greek has already made a brief appearance in these pages. For many years, ever since the Renaissance, he had played his part in the contrast as both the product of a superior culture and the purest of primitive beings. Before long his pre-Christian origins are woven into the pattern and a comparison of American Indian and Greek soon follows. Yves d'Évreux makes such a comparison as early as 1614.[88] This may have been the first delineation of the physical attributes the Indian of James Fenimore Cooper was to develop into such a celebrated model of athletic beauty, even though the athletic build forms a strange contrast to the Indian's reputedly weak physique—a subject on which a great deal of ink has been spilled ever since Las Casas. At any rate, Greek and Indian followed the same course for a time. Details of the Greeks influenced opinion on the Indian savages; the image of antiquity was colored by observation of the exotic. Three famous missionaries—Lafitau, Bufier, and Charlevoix—believed that the Homeric Greek lived on in the Indian: lost antiquity in a contemporary setting. The Indian method of bringing up their young was considered to be Spartan, while the Spartan method was found to resemble that of the Severambs.[89] Père Lafitau claimed that a few months' sojourn among the Hurons had taught him more about the Trojan War than all the lengthy works of classical scholars combined. Here, too, the historical past gained the upper hand over its mythical counterpart, and the search for a classical Lacedaemon replaced the search for Paradise. Were the autochthonous religions not Homeric in character and older than Moses or the Flood?[90] From then on Lafitau's Indians are clad in tunic or toga. When, presently, the Greek dominates the European scene (cf. Winckelmann), his new status is not solely attributable to a predilection for the classical world. The Romantics cannot forget the highly paradoxical link forged between Greek and savage.[91]

Étrangisme: belief in the absolute superiority of all things foreign; xenophilia: a new, polished form of the centuries-old pull of the primitive past preserved in contemporary reality and of the old passion for comparison. Eighteenth-century cultural and social criticism was largely based on these themes. Mohammed, Zarathustra, and Confucius all proved to be of equal worth as allies in the battle against *l'infâme*. Like Chardin, Protestantism presents Mohammed as the apostle *par excellence* of tolerance, a view which was the reverse of that of the Catholic Church. As primitivism is now defined by men such as Terrasson, cultures of a higher order hold up an admonitory finger to a Europe in process of degeneration, superseding our paradisiacal origins as the ideal against which Europe is measured. And so xenophilia is for a time the universal heir to all the old exotic primitivist and utopian themes and ideas. For that matter, the views of people like Ockley on the cultural superiority of the East were to some extent the continuation of a very old tradition. John Mandeville's Saracen Sultan had already expressed his astonishment at the Christians' dismal failure to follow the teachings of Christ. This idea, which may have originated with Mandeville, was perfected and conveyed to all parts of the world in the eighteenth century. The natural goodness that developed so harmoniously in others formed a striking contrast to our errors and corruption which—and was this not the point of Rousseau's *Discours sur l'inégalité?*—could only be seen therefore as an aberration. It could be even further refined to the point where a superior Oriental was pitted against an inferior Oriental just as the noble savage had been provided with an inferior counterpart in the figure of the *mauvais sauvage*. If the inferior Oriental was not so very different from the Westerner in his cunning and innate wickedness, the contrast revealed the noble Oriental even more clearly in the full splendor of his nobility. He is personified in Mozart's noble Pasha Selim (in *Die Entführung aus dem Serail*), whose coarse and violent harem guard showed a closer affinity to the comic interpretations of the Orient in which the seventeenth century had sometimes taken such delight (cf. Molière). The contrast between the noble Oriental and the European was thrown into even sharper relief.

Something of the same situation had already been apparent in *Floire et Blanceflor*. Despite his playfulness, however, Mozart's version comes closer to the actual roots of human behavior. To begin with, Selim is a psychologically acceptable figure. Secondly, it is neither an upsurge of amiability, cheap sentimentality, nor easy-going friendliness which moves him to be merciful to the deceivers, the young nobleman Belmonte and his beloved Constanze. In order to introduce the human element—highlighting Eastern noblesse rather than the dazzling bizarreness of an exotic fairy-tale world—Mozart devised real complications, thereby deviating from the story on which his opera was based. It transpires that Belmonte, the Floire of the eighteenth century, is not only the abductor of the Pasha's beloved and the intruder in his harem; he is also the son of his most deadly enemy. It is precisely this exceptional circumstance, however, of which both men were at first unaware, that gives the Pasha the unique opportunity of showing himself to be the superior Oriental.* Not only does he forgive Belmonte for the outrage—in accordance with the old formula—and restore his Constanze to him, but his motives for this decision are infinitely superior to those of the twelfth-century Admiral of Babylon and his cordial harem guard. "Sail to your fatherland; tell your father that you were in my power, that I re-

---

*Fact and fancy: the musicologist Jacob once hit upon the happy idea of taking a Turk to a performance of the *Entführung,* asking his opinion of the *alla turca* motifs inserted by Mozart to create an oriental atmosphere. The Turk, however, recognized nothing Turkish in the music; he found it completely Western, and his opinion is borne out by the examples of Turkish music which Jacob then proceeds to give. Heinrich Eduard Jacob, *Mozart, Geist, Musik und Schicksal* [Dutch translation: *Mozart, mysterie-engenade,* ed. Brima, trans. Johan le Molenaaz (Utrecht, 1956), p. 243].

leased you so that you could tell him [the Pasha is an object lesson in clemency for all peoples] that it is a far greater pleasure [indeed, it is more than just a matter of virtue, of duty coming first; it is actually a pleasure] to reward iniquity with mercy than to repay wickedness with wickedness." Of course this is an exceptional example. It surpasses Gluck's King Thoas (in the opera *Iphigenia in Aulis*) as it also surpasses Goethe's Thoas (in his *Iphigenia auf Tauris*) who gives Iphigenia and Orestes their freedom, but not before it has been necessary to employ a great deal of Western persuasiveness. Mozart, on the other hand, raises the Oriental to a position which is perhaps equaled only in Lessing's drama, *Nathan der Weise*—a monument of eighteenth-century humanitarian philosophy.

The complex of motives involved in European man's relation to non-European man and his world is intricate. The dichotomy of the European soul is an essential part of that complex. The strands of myth and political reality that cross and recross are too closely interwoven ever to be disentangled. They represent not irreconcilable truth and falsehood, but rather two separate truths, each of which claims an absolute right to sole supremacy. But in only a few exceptional periods in history was one of them in a position to enforce its claims and obtain complete ascendancy over its rival. The glorification of the red Indian, and of the noble savage in general, deeply influenced European expansion to the west in the sixteenth and seventeenth centuries, but it failed to prevent the wholesale massacres that accompanied this expansion. The myths covered the distant earthly paradises with a veil of enchantment through which they were seen as the home of the blessed and the elect, but they formed no hindrance to their intensive and ruthless economic exploitation. Political expediency stimulated and controlled all the discoveries and expeditions from the famous Portuguese conquest of Ceuta in 1415 onward, but none of these undertakings shook themselves free of their mystical roots, as evidenced by the enduring vitality of so many mythical interpretations. Finally, the eighteenth century was very much the century of rationalism—of skepticism and the *Encyclopédie*—but it failed to prevent romanticism, sentiment, and exoticism with all their inner contradictions from exerting a great deal of influence on Europe's relations with the outside world.

This fundamental duality also conditioned the eighteenth century's approach to the non-Western world. There was, on the one hand, the actual physical outside world which could be put to political, economic, and strategic use; there was also the outside world onto which all identification and interpretation, all dissatisfaction and desire, all nostalgia and idealism seeking expression could be projected. And although one of these two worlds may have been circumscribed by fixed, material circumstances, the other remained infinitely variable, infinitely interpretable, adjusting itself with endless patience to all the twists and turns of our thought.

The full flowering of exoticism in the eighteenth century was not the whim of a playful period; it was the expression of a fundamental element in our culture. It was a predominant form of thought in an era that was seriously yet superficially interested in self-analysis and self-criticism. The whole complex of the new primitivism, and of orientalism in particular, undoubtedly contained a substantial element of rejection and renunciation—not of life but of a civilization that was felt to be both a burden and a path leading in the wrong direction. Is primitivism then the forerunner of a crisis? And perhaps of revolution? Was it the precursor of that famous protest against history, the revolutionary creed of 1789 claiming that *tout est à refaire* and advocating the total demolition of everything as an essential prerequisite for shaping a new history, a new culture, and a new society? Should that protest be seen as deriving from man's dissatisfaction with the world in which he lives, a dissatisfaction he had already sought to assuage so many centuries earlier in his search for his mythical, paradisiacal past and, later, in his myth-inspired speculations regarding the unknown, outside world? Did the American War of Independence go hand in hand with a strong revival of Indianophilia; did the

55

colonists, who wished to establish a new state and a new society, identify themselves to a certain extent with the Indians who had at one time pitted themselves against European covetousness? This has been claimed—and contradicted. But however that may be, the attackers of the celebrated tea ship in Boston in 1773 were disguised as Indians. Denis Brogan has drawn attention to the tendency to glorify the peasant that preceded the Russian Revolution of 1917, reminiscent of the eighteenth century's predilection for the rustic, the idyllic, and the pastoral. The Physiocrats fit into this picture. And near the Petit Trianon Marie Antoinette, the unfortunate queen, had her *hameau,* the farm where she and the ladies of the Court played at milkmaids. Those who, like Seillière, trace the roots of the new awareness of the lower, the "primitive," social classes to the primitivism of the eighteenth century are involuntarily reminded of Renan's statement that social ideas have a disintegrating effect and activate hostility to culture, and that herein lies a sort of eternal tragedy of history. Does this correspond to what Burckhardt meant when he spoke of "the central phenomenon of history"?[92]

Once these links, with all their strange implications, have been established, it is easy to correlate them with Burckhardt's reflections on a similar phenomenon in fourth-century Greece. At first, the Greeks' self-awareness was determined by the contrast they provided with the barbarian world, even though their feeling of superiority was not founded on indisputable fact. But about the fourth century this contrast, which had always been central to the argument, evaporated rather suddenly, an event that may have been influenced by the inter-Hellenic wars or by the gradual wasting away of that feeling of cohesion and belonging together which, in spite of everything, had always been shared by the various Greek states. Or it may have been influenced by the philosophical ideas of the Cynics and, more especially, of the Stoics who saw the Hellenes and the barbarians, collectively, as children of God.[93] A century after Alexander and the birth of Alexandrian exoticism, Eratosthenes rejected all distinction between good people and bad people: "for many Hellenes are morally corrupt and many barbarians are morally noble like the Indians and the Aryans, and also Romans and Carthaginians, are good." Still earlier, largely in Sparta, an Egyptophilia belonging to the same order of phenomenon had appeared, influencing both Plato and Isocrates. Burckhardt likened this eulogizing of Egypt, which contrasted so strangely with the contempt in which non-Hellenic peoples were generally held, to the leanings of the Enlightenment toward China.[94] Finally, a further decisive step was taken, the outcome of which was a feat of rationalization not unworthy of our own century: if the barbarians are wicked then the Greeks must have corrupted them, since the barbarians are virtuous and the Greeks are godless.[95] This seems to clash with the traditional Greek view of themselves: that their culture had transcended barbarousness and turned away from Asia—the Persians, the East, in short the non-Greek world—to arrive at the heights that were its unique characteristic. The earlier inspiring belief in the natural superiority of culture to barbarousness referred to by Burckhardt is thus provided with a strange counterbalance in a preference for the exotic that ends in self-accusation. No rational explanation would seem to be adequate; it must be supplemented by another sort of logic. Has civilization wearied of itself? Why, then, is it weary and what is the nature of this weariness that coincides with such creativeness? Has it lost the capacity to carry excess cultural baggage? Then why is that capacity reduced? It would seem, in any case, that a longing for simplification and simplicity remains dormant until the advent of a period of weakened resistance, when it breaks through in one form or another. The Romans display analogous phenomena from the third century A.D. onward. And ever since Gibbon established a connection between the decline of the Roman Empire and the rise and expansion of Christianity—that

57

strange, new Levantine religion—historians have tied many of their interpretations of the fall of Rome to this or to a similar phenomenon. Nearly a century after Gibbon, Fustel de Coulanges still regarded Tacitus' description of the Germanic peoples as pure observation; we are inclined to perceive a strain of xenophilia as well, a trait shared by others writing in the first centuries of the empire such as Ovid, Seneca, and Lucan. Here again one is forced to think in terms of sentiments which are always in existence but which vary in intensity with the centuries.

For the image of a lost Paradise and its accompanying nostalgia for vanished halcyon days are universal phenomena. Anthropologists tell us that it is known to all peoples.[96] A catastrophe brought our original ideal state to an end. All historical thought thus seems, in principle, to be degenerative. In the beginning, in the Golden Age, there was, by definition, no history. Adam did not begin to think historically, in terms of the past, until he had been driven out of Paradise. While still in Paradise he did think of the future: one of God's first commands to him was to multiply himself. Procreation is the future. But history, does it only begin to exist when there is a past to remember, to lament, and to idealize? And did the Great Revolution of 1789, with its long previous history, wish to find the way back to Paradise so that history could then begin anew, this time without the Fall and the Expulsion? This ideal was more than the wild dream of an overwrought brain like Rousseau's: in his *Lettres Persanes* Montesquieu spoke of the blissfully happy Troglodytes who, having been brought low by their vices, were guided back to a state of virtue, justice, and natural purity (both socially and economically) by two of their kind. The history of the Troglodytes then began anew, as it were, and they created a new and happy egalitarian and communist society. Marat was deeply impressed by this story, and the astute Diderot scarcely less so.[97]

58

Kant, probing further below the surface, saw ambition, greed, and miserliness, all asocial and antisocial characteristics, to be historical prerequisites for man's emergence from his original stage of savagery.[98] Of course the Troglodytes were by definition just as Western as the imagination from which they sprang. After all, the whole story took place in Montesquieu's study. But this is still another reason for recognizing it as a perfect expression of the synthesis of projection-onto-the-past and projection-onto-the-outside-world so characteristic of our culture.

Usbek's letters to Mirza on the Troglodytes united the two fundamental aspects of the myth of a better world in a harmony seldom equaled. The theme of turning away from one's own society and culture now assumed a completely European form. Economic freedom, defined as social equality based on the division of labor and private property, and man's proximity to nature coupled with his prehistoric past[99] (the man and woman starting afresh)—these are the components of the mythical element in the European conception of itself and of the outside world. The image was first projected onto the European and his past, then it was projected onto non-Western peoples who, "not yet" corrupt like the European, were "still" in the practically paradisiacal state we may or may not have lost forever. Finally, the two images were fused into a single universal image of human existence throughout the length and breadth of the earth.

World history was born at that moment and, since it is based on a philosophical rather than an historical principle, it is still the philosophers rather than the historians who write it.[100] Its birth certificate bears the signature of both the old myth and the new social philosophy: in Burckhardt's words, "Speculative thought made its appearance in the guise of a creator of new political forms, but actually as a general solvent, at first in words, which inevitably lead to deeds." World history is a child of the century that protested against history, the century that was unhistorical on principle. To quote Burckhardt again, "for history . . . is unphilosophical and philosophy is . . . unhistorical."[100a]

Does this explain why the nineteenth century—the century that realized its ambition to become an historical century *par excellence*—failed to pursue the course laid down by eighteenth-century universalism? Or why the historians turned away from *Nichtgeschichte*—philosophy—abandoning it and the mythology that supported it to the poets and the novelists, the philosophers and the orientalists? There is no doubt that historical thought in the nineteenth century deliberately restricted itself to a limited field of vision which did not include non-European peoples and cultures—it barely encompassed the European ones. After all, history should be national history; it should be patriotic. It should form a link between what Thierry calls "our forefathers as they were and us as we are" and, above all, it should have nothing to do with the philosophical digressions of the eighteenth century.[101] This view was opposed to any form of philosophical *abstraction de l'histoire* as well as to *la version monarchique de l'histoire* (of France).[102] For the new nineteenth-century myth is the nation; before long this is to be narrowed down to the people as a group in that nation. History now becomes a record of their oppression and resistance as English history was a record of the struggle between the Norman invaders and the oppressed Saxons[103] or—to give a living example—as Greece was making history at that moment (1825) in its furious resistance to the Turks. National history held up a picture of a slow advance through the ages toward freedom, *la liberté du peuple dans le sens politique du mot.*[104]

The definition of the word *peuple* became the key to and the point of departure for the study of history.[105] That explains why the early nineteenth century was so medievalist and at the same time so absorbed in the overwhelming events of 1789.

Often, in these days, the rise and progress of the people [wrote Michelet] are compared to the invasion of the *Barbarians*. The expression pleases me; I accept it. *Barbarians!* Yes, that is to say, full of new, living, regenerating sap. *Barbarians,* that is, travellers marching towards the Rome of the future, going on slowly, doubtless; each generation advancing a little, halting in death; but others march forward all the same. We other Barbarians have a natural advantage; if the upper classes have culture, we have much more vital heat (nous avons bien plus de chaleur vitale).[106]

Unlike Thierry, Michelet does not exclude all other groups from the nation although for him too the true France is the France of the Great Revolution.[107]

Freedom and progress are the dominant themes of national history outside France as well, even in countries where interpretation of the terms "people" and "nation" differs from the passionate French version. Pieter Geyl quotes a significant passage from Macaulay which penetrates to the heart of the matter:

The history of England is emphatically the history of progress . . . Each of those great and ever-memorable struggles, Saxon against Norman, Villein against Lord, Protestant against Papist, Roundhead against Cavalier, Dissenter against Churchman, Manchester against Old Sarum, was, in its own order and season, a struggle, on the result of which were staked the dearest interests of the human race; and every man who, in the contest which, in his time, divided our country, distinguished himself on the right side, is entitled to our gratitude and respect.[108]

Or else, like Fruin, one could relate freedom and progress to the destiny of the House of Orange.[109]

61

The fundamental belief shared by so many nineteenth-century historians was that history was national both in form and content. History to them was first and foremost the history, the growth, of their own nation; it was conceded, however, that there could be such a thing as a European process of growth (cf. Ranke).[110] But there was no place here for the non-European world unless it served the interests of the national idea. By *die Welt* Ranke meant Europe; Michelet's *le monde entier* and *l'humanité*[111] comprised—in addition to France—England, Germany, Scotland, Ireland, and perhaps Italy. James Mill, the father of John Stuart Mill, showed no awareness of anything much beyond the British element in his *History of India,* a work hailed by Macaulay as a fine example of historical writing in the new style.[112]

And so the effervescent sentiment of the early nineteenth century produces a view of history shot through with a cheerful optimism. Concealing itself in no degenerative shadows, it expresses a firm belief in the continuing growth of national life and in the ultimate perfection of national expression. The paradises envisaged by the new history are no longer derived from exotic worlds or from painful feelings of nostalgia for a lost happiness. On returning from Egypt, Napoleon said that he was disgusted with Rousseau and all his noble savages: *L'homme sauvage est un chien.*[113] The nineteenth century, or at any rate its historians, reacted to its predecessor with bold self-assurance. The fact of national superiority was self-evident, and the fact of Western superiority would have been deemed equally self-evident, in the very nature of things, had it occurred to anyone to draw comparisons. But this did not happen, and by the time a variety of factors obliged the comparison to be made in the second half of the century the new reality of the intensive colonization of overseas territories coincided with a sensational upward curve of the lines of production and achievement, as was demonstrated by the great exhibitions which took place in rapid succession after the

Crystal Palace Exhibition of 1851.[114] The colonial sections of the international exhibitions furnished convincing proof of European world power bent on scaling even more distant peaks. There was no reason why complacent self-confidence should give way to gloomier feelings.

But when pessimism appears just the same—even manifesting itself in an almost deterministic form—and makes its dissenting voice heard, it is still not the eighteenth-century or earlier comparison with exotic peoples and worlds that leads to a negative assessment of European culture and its future. No external, comparative considerations can be held responsible for the gloomy view commented on so discerningly by Geyl.[115] De Tocqueville began to notice the predominance of the new revolutionary dialectic summed up so brilliantly by Denis Brogan when he stated that after 1776—the American Declaration of Independence—revolution acquired the status of an institution in our society.[116] Taine believed that rapidly evolving democracy could not fail to magnify the worst aspects of man and society and would lead to degeneration. But in complete contrast to the gloom which in the previous century had gone hand in hand with a firm belief in progress, it did not seem to the nineteenth century that either a fundamental degeneration or a mistaken blueprint for civilization would bring about the decay of Western man; nineteenth-century pessimism was caused by certain developments which it rejected and which from a certain point onward threatened to steer an otherwise sound cause into the wrong channels. Even outside France, the revolutionary temper of the century—1776, 1789, and all that these years had brought in their wake—was usually at the heart of these misgivings.[117] It caused a deep and prolonged rift in contemporary thought, dividing thinkers into those who subscribed to the myth of the revolution and those who rejected it.

The nature of the rift, however, was strictly Western. In European eyes, the American Revolution was part of European history. No thoughts of non-European worlds entered this picture; even the South American mestizo revolution, which finally led to the emergence of all those independent republics, was not seen as a conflict between the Western and non-Western worlds.[118] Spanish America simply became Latin America. "Every race and every land which has been successively romanized, christianized, and subjected in intellectual matters to the discipline of the Greeks, is absolutely European."[119]

Did this mean that the myths of primitivism now faded altogether from the gaze of the nineteenth century even though something of them was passed on to the poets and philosophers?[120] Was Chateaubriand's complaint about the *philosophes nus* (*Les Natchez*) and our inability to return to their primitive state at the most an echo of an old melody and not even a faint prelude to a nineteenth-century theme? Should Sénancour's *Rêverie,*[121] written on the threshold of the nineteenth century, be interpreted as no more than a dying echo of Lafitau, an integral part of the preceding rather than the following era?

The new generation of Romantics found new themes. The noble savage is unknown to Hugo and Scott, and the latter's Saladin cannot be mistaken for one. Western progress is the dominant theme and the myth of primitivism makes no headway until the perennially dissenting voice is raised against the optimistic view of progress in the second half of the century. Does this century sound, after all, a completely different note from that of any other period? Is the European's relation to the non-European subject to the new world law of Western supremacy? The dissenting voice may sound a warning, give evidence of dejection or insight into imminent danger, but nothing suggests any sort of European inferiority to the outside worlds of Asia and Africa (America and Australia being European). Cultural rejection is not a nineteenth-century theme. True, it rejected the spirit of 1789, the spirit of the

64

Great Revolution; like Balzac, Flaubert, and Bourget, like Zola, Taine, Renan,[122] and Schopenhauer—all of whom were *pessimistes en psychologie, optimistes en moral,* as Seillière advised us to be[123]—and it was perhaps somber in its attitude to man and humanity. Nineteenth-century social romantics may have protested against a social structure based on the new techniques and the new economy,[124] and may have adopted slogans of reform, but no part of their rejection, somberness, and slogan-making seems to me to have had the intention of extolling the virtues of any outside world to the detriment of Europe. "Oh let these last sons of nature die out in their mother's lap; do not interrupt, with your austere dogmas the fruit of twenty centuries of reflection, their childish games, their moonlight dances, their sweet though ephemeral raptures,"[125] wrote the young Renan in what was still an unswerving belief in the cultural superiority of the West. Insofar as the nineteenth century did develop a specific exoticism— the American Indian novel, the Crusoe cult, novels of the South Seas, Stevenson, Conrad, Loti, Gauguin, Ewers and Hesse, Kipling's *Jungle Book*—it seldom seems to be directed against the country or continent of origin.

And the infant socialism, for all its protests, did not at first distinguish itself by adopting a different attitude toward the non-Western world. It was abolitionist, desiring the abolition of slavery, but its demands in this respect were no longer attuned to the current situation. It advocated a form of protection for the peoples of the colonies (*qu'on élève progressivement les indigènes*[126]) but it was by no means the sole advocate of this view. The main point is that, subject to these conditions, socialism regarded the expansion and colonization which were now developing at a rapid pace as events of worldwide importance, an opinion fully consonant with the commonly held view of the non-Western world, where Western supremacy was the undisputed cornerstone of historical and even biological evolution. It did not allow much scope for

65

thoughts of degeneration and Paradise lost. The young eth-
nologists and the new study of prehistory fitted perfectly into
this climate of thought. They erected a monument to a mankind that had been marching onward for countless centuries
and would, with the West at its head, eventually scale the cultural heights.

But a change took place, and at the Socialist Congress held
at Paris in 1900 a dispossessed and destitute colored man
found himself in the company of the European proletarian,
as proclaimed by Van Kol and Hyndman.[127] It then became
apparent that the long absence of the old myth of the natural
goodness of man, especially of the dispossessed and those who
had not undergone the corrupting influence of culture, had
been no more than a superficial optical illusion. In the new
social constellation of Europe there was again room for the
myth of a golden past and perhaps even of a golden future,
with the present as a dark valley devoid of all prospect lying
somewhere between the two. The *pauvre sauvage* was the obvious figure to share the plight of the European proletarian in
that valley. They were both the children of God referred to in
the Sermon on the Mount. They were both destined to reach
loftier heights. And the fundamental dividing line is no longer
between Western and non-Western man but cuts right across
all continents, separating the good people (and the dispossessed
in particular) from the wicked. The good in all parts of the
world, whether Christian or not, belong together in this image
in an almost Augustinian way, and their ultimate reward in a
still shadowy future is as certain as was that of the Children
of Light to the Latin Christianity of the Middle Ages.

Good and bad are now to be found on both sides of the
ancient line that had separated Europe from the outside world.
A century ago the Dutch writer Multatuli expressed it most
forcefully: it is the concept which Max Havelaar, the central
figure in his book, voices in his impassioned plea to protect
the humble Javanese from their more highly placed com-

66

patriots by means of more rather than less Western intervention, *provided* a distinction be made between good and bad Europeans employed for the purpose. Karl May provides yet another striking, albeit differently structured, example.[128] In this case it was an image that made such a strong appeal. His Old Shatterhand is the white savior, the one who knows all, dares all, and never fails to accomplish his purpose. He is fluent in all languages and dialects, and the Apaches, whose prisoner he is at first, are swayed by a natural respect for all these superb qualities and have not only not harmed him in any way but have made him a sort of honorary chief. He is the brother of Winnetou, himself a splendid portrayal of the noble savage of the nineteenth century. Infinitely superior to the average Indian, he is an exception of the highest order. And that is very much the point: Karl May's savages bear a closer resemblance to those of Defoe than to those of Rousseau. For —another point which echoes Defoe—there are other Indians besides the upright Apaches. There are noble Indians and there are wicked Indians like the Sioux tribes. But though Karl May (unlike the Socialists) rejects Rousseau's myth, he too draws a dividing line between good and bad which cuts across both Indian and European societies. Moreover, just as the good and bad qualities of his Indian society are associated with certain tribes, he recognizes two types of European: the good European is always German (Old Shatterhand, Old Firehand, and others) while the villain is English or, more often, French (Thibaud-taka and Thibaud-wete).[129] In the strange contrast revealed by the somewhat unusual comparison of Max Havelaar with Old Shatterhand, each figure represents a myth. They are contrasting myths: the myth of primitivism as against the myth of nationalism. The first passes a negative judgment on our civilization and glorifies primitive worlds; the second sees only virtues in the nation and vices in the foreign world. Are they not the two myths that sum up the century now drawing to a close?

The legendary Old Shatterhand is a true representative of a highly developed West in the non-Western world. He is no longer filled with nostalgia for a lost Paradise; the practical aspects of contact between the white and colored races are now the principal theme. For all his limited vision, Karl May nevertheless stated the problem as it actually existed for the progressive thinkers of his time, who were faced with the problem of bridging the gap between lower and higher cultures. The great explorers and empire builders—the Stanleys, the Rhodeses, the Galliénis, the Lyauteys, and so many others, including in some ways De Lesseps—displayed an undeniable similarity with Karl May's legendary woodsman. For one thing they also developed personal ties with the colored peoples whom they got to know and who, in turn, were impressed by them. Jameson said of Rhodes, whose personal physician and life-long friend he was: "[He] was really, by nature, strongly and deeply in sympathy with the natives."[130] Like Old Shatterhand, they too drew the inevitable distinction between good savages (who, like the Apaches, were well disposed) and bad savages (who remained hostile). And, like him, they applied the same standards to national relations in Europe. With the possible exception of Stanley, they were all mystics. Rhodes harbored a mystical belief in England's mission to rule black Africa and the whole world. Lyautey had a no less firm conviction that France was destined not to rule but to civilize.[131] De Lesseps was obsessed by a pronounced mystic feeling that his personal mission was to realize an almost un-nineteenth-century universalist aim: the unification of Europe and Asia as symbolized by the rainbow he had seen near Suez and had interpreted as a divine revelation. Stanley's view, however, was different. What he saw were the immense riches Africa promised to yield to its ruler. "Who wishes to civilize Africa? Who wishes to open the trade direct with Usagara, Useguhha, Ukutu, Uhehe; to get the ivory, the sugar, the cotton, the orchilla weed, the indigo, and the grain of these countries?

Here is an opportunity!"[132] These considerations ranked with the two myths, constituting a third basic theme.

At this point I wish to cite a little-read and almost forgotten page from the wise Renan, who tried to find a solution to the problem in 1878 when he wrote a sort of sequel to Shakespeare's *Tempest*.[133] Here again we find the black Caliban, Prospero, and Ariel. Is Caliban the authentic *sauvage* that Ariel takes him for? Is he not rather the representative of a different culture, one that is real and exotic at the same time? He is, in any case, the non-European who has come into contact with and been changed by Western culture. The scene is therefore shifted to Pavia whither Prospero, "sure of being the instrument of a searching will" (he has obeyed an inner, mystic urge), has transported his savage. He has made Caliban a member of his court; he has civilized him—who wishes to civilize?—and provided him with a post (a minor post, to be sure, but a post nevertheless). But the former savage is bitter at the loss of his freedom and his enchanted isle.

> *Ariel:* Why dost thou revolt? . . . Possibly in freedom thou mightst be less happy than now.
>
> *Caliban:* Yes, but I am simply another man's tool, his machine to work upon. Base valet, dost thou not see, then, that being experimented upon by another is the most insupportable of things? . . .
>
> *Ariel:* Thou forgettest that thou owest thy manhood and existence to Prospero.
>
> *Caliban:* That is fine logic. But the island was mine. I was there before him, and it belonged to me through my mother. The fertile fields, the abundant springs, the goodly trees which went to Prospero were all mine, and he has only given me in return this slavery.
>
> *Ariel:* Thou sayest without cessation that the island belonged to thee. In truth, it did belong to thee, just as the desert belongs to the gazelle, the jungle to the tiger,

and no more. Thou knewest the name of nothing there. Thou wast a stranger to reason and thy inarticulate language resembled the bellowing of an angry camel more than any human speech . . . Prospero taught thee the Aryan language, and with that divine tongue the channel of reason has become inseparable from thee. Little by little, thanks to language and reason, thy deformed features have become harmonized, thy web-fingers have separated themselves one from the other, and from a poisonous fish thou hast become a man. Even now thou speakest almost like a son of Italy.

Caliban: Oh! Be silent thou! The language in itself answers me well enough. Why did not Prospero see that the Aryan tongue which he taught me I would use as a means by which to curse him? He is an idiot . . . I am indebted to Prospero for everything thou sayest. He was unwise. Were I in his place I would not have done so . . . Ingratitude is the stamp of humanity. Every effort to elevate another person reacts against the educator. Each lives according to his character. The crocodile only has a great mouth with which to better provide for his sustenance. As cursing is my nature, I cannot curb my invectives. To give me a language was to equip me for that end.

That is how the mature Renan summarized the basic themes of which he had been unaware in his youth but which he now recognized as the crux of the colonial question. First and foremost, there is Ariel: he rides on the clouds and is not of this earth, but for this very reason he can try to see everything in its entirety—not only the divine right of culture as opposed to barbarism (Burckhardt), but the humanitarian meaning as well. Secondly, there is Caliban: the savage who is experiencing the full import of the Western urge for advancement and civilization. There is the enchanted isle with the economic significance of its fields, wells, and orchards. Finally, there is Prospero, the figure who of course holds the most interest for us: the Westerner who voyaged over the seas, who was fated to discover Caliban's island, and who came into contact with its population. After exploring the new-found country, he took over its exploitation at the suggestion of Caliban himself. But above all, "sure of being the instrument of a searching will"— let us remember that!—he has assumed by way of "exchange" the role of guardian, educator, and benefactor in the way considered by a protectively inclined West to be best suited to philanthropic deeds. That is the combination of old urge and new emancipation theory as it is to be effected, after Renan, by men such as Paul Leroy-Beaulieu, Jules Harmand, and, to some extent, by Van Vollenhoven, who was so profoundly influenced by Renan.[134] And so, whether the idea was termed assimilation, association, or adaptation, Prospero is a personification of the European of the new era, with the one essential difference that the scene of his activities is set, after all, in his European duchy. He is not the type of colonizing Westerner whose relation to the outside world is determined by a reality devoid of all respect for philosophy. He is not the colonizing Westerner to whom Kipling addressed his famous words at the end of the century:

> Take up the White Man's burden,
> Send forth the best ye breed,
> Go bind your sons to exile,
> To serve your captives' need . . .

But in another way Prospero is a European of the era that Renan saw approaching with the new century, the main themes of whose history he recorded in the prophetic second part of his drama. For the people rise in revolt against Prospero, who wished to rule his country wisely (Act II, scene 1); then their unconstrained bitterness toward their monarch, who had wanted only good, joins forces with the hatred expressed by Caliban in the opening dialogue. Caliban, like the people them-

71

selves, is the pitiable victim of the régime and its *volonté*. But there is no longer any question of a dialogue between him and Ariel, the sprite not of this world. Instead, the emancipated savage makes an impassioned appeal to the rebellious populace (Act II, scene 1). He sums up the theory of revolution in trenchant phrases anathematizing Prospero's class, intellect, and culture, together with his books and the Latin in which he is proficient and which to Caliban is symbolic of his power. His convictions are couched in the language of reason learned from Prospero, a language which he now employs in the service of the new revolutionary reason.

> The blame of those ye better,
> The hate of those ye guard . . .

It is no more than a short step from here to the movement that will proclaim him *chef du peuple, l'homme de la situation,* and, investing him with full authority, will make him master of the duchy. Since the masses are gripped by the myth, the Negro Caliban must be superior to all Europeans in insight, in ingenuity, in strength, and in moderation—in short, in all virtues and talents. "He is ugly, but how well he reasons!" (Act IV, scene 4). And those who are perhaps not impressed by the myth still find it to their own advantage to fall cynically into line behind the new ruler, supporting the new social relationships that now emerge and the theory—"speculative thought as the universal solvent" of which Burckhardt spoke[135] —that has made it imperative to reexamine all the old values. This means reexamining, above all, Prospero's right to rule Milan and Pavia; it means, furthermore, his right to Caliban's magic island together with all that this implies. Finally, it means belief in a divine mission to protect Kipling's "silent sullen peoples." It is these old, basic creeds that the violence of the fourth estate, the populace of Milan, is sweeping away as though by a tidal wave: the tidal wave of the ancient myth of Western inferiority.

The government of Louis-Philippe, the king who had also made a vain attempt to pursue the good, and the revolutions of 1848 were plainly the background to Renan's drama. But extending the problem of 1848, he transformed it into one common to the whole of Europe. The relation of monarch to people was now the psychological relation of the West to the masses of the non-Western world. Renan, an orientalist at heart who was accustomed to making constant comparisons between European and non-European realities, saw the new revolutionary logic of the nineteenth-century West as a world-wide problem for the next century.[136] He anticipated an enormous conflict between old practice and new theory or, as Prospero stated when summoned to appear before the Papal Court, "Let them work on empty abstractions, and I will work on realities."[137]

EPILOGUE

From the gateway to the twentieth century we return to our point of departure, having discovered in the course of our long journey that the relation of European to non-European man seems, on the whole, to be governed by two factors, each of which functions independently of the other. One is determined by material facts in the way in which relations can usually be determined by facts. The other, at once more intensive and more compelling, is bred by an inner urge that does not stem from objective facts—gold, silver, spices, etc.—but from nostalgia for the deep, the ideal, the ultimate harmony still cherished as the real purpose of the Creation. That remembrance accompanied Adam when he was driven forth from Paradise and is referred to in the famous Adam apocrypha, "The Treasure-Cave." And that same remembrance may have been the beginning of our sense of history.

At first, our culture thought of that harmony in terms of *time,* seeking it in our own or in another "absolute" past. This was the true, the regrettably lost Paradise that became the cradle of our degeneration, but that Christ again restored to our view. Remembrance and projections of the future thus gaining a new identity, the cycle was complete.

In a following era, however, that perfect harmony was sought in terms of *space:* in a real or nonexistent contemporary world; all outside worlds that appealed to the imagination became identified with it to some extent.

With the eighteenth century in mind, one might state that the less a period thought in *historical* terms, the more it stressed contemporary expectations of perfect happiness and identi-

74

fied these expectations with the contemporary world. That might explain why the eighteenth century, with its protesting attitude toward the whole of history—an attitude also displayed to some extent by our own century—felt so strongly attracted to the other world known or thought to exist outside Europe. And it might also explain the universalism that went with it.

Continuing this train of thought, perhaps it may be claimed that the more a century (the nineteenth century for example) was historically orientated, the less inclined it was to think in universalist terms and, in consequence, to seek Paradise beyond the horizon. It is not my contention that dreams of this sort were unknown to the nineteenth century. Endless nostalgia is not wholly alien to any period, but it has tended to be more dominant in some than in others.

My simile of two lines on which all the different parts of the theme appear to be arranged seems to me to be the best means of approaching the problem. Culture, like the individual, seems to exist on two different levels: the level of real and imagined remembrance which can evolve into nostalgia for simplicity as it was in the beginning,[138] and the level of actual experience in an ever-continuous reality. But in response to an absolute condition for survival, the two seem to be fused into an indissoluble unity, an inextricably interwoven complex of myth and reality.

And that is precisely our dilemma.

NOTES

Note: Wherever possible, English translations have been added or substituted for works originally cited by the author in other languages.

1. René Grousset: *Histoire des croisades et du royaume franc de Jérusalem* (Paris, Plon, 1935); *Bilan de l'histoire* (Paris, Plon, 1946), p. 235 [A. H. Patterson, *The Sum of History* (Hadleigh, Essex, Tower Bridge, 1951), p. 192]; *L'homme et son histoire* (Paris, Plon, 1954).

2. Christopher Dawson, *The Making of Europe* (London, Sheed and Ward, 1932). Is the paradox of this mixed character fully expressed in the Iliad? It is Paris—the Trojan, the Asian— who has abducted the Greek queen of Sparta. But in Homer's epic of the war waged by the Greeks in retaliation for this outrage (which lacked justification even on the ground of passion) the blind poet's sympathies are still on the side of Asia. The Asian Hector is, at any rate, the incarnation of true nobility in the midst of the rough Trojans and Greeks. Later, Vergil carries the theme further in Aeneas—pious Aeneas—and the Middle Ages continue the trend. See also A. E. Cohen, *De visie op Troje van de Westerse middeleeuwse geschiedschrijvers tot 1160* (Assen, Van Gorcum, 1941), and bibliography.

3. André Siegfried, *Voyage aux Indes* (Paris, Colin, 1951), pp. 153 and 92.

4. Pieter Geyl, *Encounters in History* (London, Collins, 1963), p. 357.

5. Mircea Eliade, *Mythes, rêves, mystères* (Paris, Gallimard, 1957), p. 18 [Philip Mairet, *Myths, Dreams, and Mysteries* (New York, Harper, 1960)].

6. Pieter Geyl, *Use and Abuse of History* (New Haven, Yale University Press, 1955), p. 63.

7. Ernest Seillière: *Introduction à la philosophie de l'impéria-*

lisme (Paris, Alcan, 1911); *Mysticisme et domination* (Paris, Alcan, 1913); *L'impérialisme démocratique* (Paris, Plon-Nourrit, 1907); *Le romantisme et la morale* (Paris, La Nouvelle revue critique, 1932); *Le romantisme et la politique* (Paris, La Nouvelle revue critique, 1932).

8. George Boas and Arthur O. Lovejoy, eds., *A Documentary History of Primitivism and Related Ideas* (Baltimore, Johns Hopkins Press, 1935).

9. Jean Bodin, *Methodus, ad facilem historiarum cognitionem* (Paris, 1566, 2d ed. 1572). See J. B. Bury, *The Idea of Progress: An Inquiry into Its Origin and Growth* (London, Macmillan, 1920), pp. 37–39.

10. Robert H. Lowie, *The History of Ethnological Theory* (New York, Farrar and Rinehart, 1937), pp. 4–5.

11. George Boas, *Essays on Primitivism and Related Ideas in the Middle Ages* (Baltimore, Johns Hopkins Press, 1948), p. 137.

12. Gomes Eannes de Azurara, *Chronicon of the Discovery and Conquest of Guinea,* ed. Charles Beazly and Edgar Prestage (London, Hakluyt Society, 1896), p. 7.

13. Pierre Martino, *L'orient dans la littérature française au XVIIe et au XVIIIe siècle* (Paris, Hachette, 1906), Introduction. Europe long remained ignorant of the origin of the many articles obtained through trade with the Islamic world.

14. René Grousset, *L'homme et son histoire,* p. 234.

15. Frederik C. Wieder, *Monumenta cartographica* (The Hague, Nijhoff, 1925–33); Boies Penrose, *Travel and Discovery in the Renaissance, 1420–1620* (Cambridge, Mass., Harvard University Press, 1952); Joachim G. Leithäuser, *Mappae mundi* (Berlin, Safari-Verlag, 1958); Richard Hennig, *Terrae incognitae: Eine Zusammensetzung und kritische Bewertung der wichtigsten vorcolumbischen Entdeckungsreisen* (2 vols. Leiden, Brill, 1944–56); Konrad Miller, *Mappaemundi: die ältesten Weltkarten* (Stuttgart, Roth, 1895–98). See bibliography in L. Bagrow, *Die Geschichte der Kartographie* (Berlin, Safari-Verlag, 1951).

16. Hans Plischke, *Die Völker Europas und das Zeitalter der Entdeckungen* (Bremen, A. Geist, 1943), p. 13.

17. Pierre D. Huet, *A Treatise of the Situation of Paradise,* trans. Thomas Gale (London, printed for J. Knapton, 1694). See Arturo Graf, *Miti, leggende e supersitizioni del medio evo* (Torino, E. Loescher, 1892–93).

18. Boas, *Essays on Primitivism,* pp. 154 ff.

19. Luis Vaz de Camoens, *The Luisad,* trans. R. Fanshawe, ed. J. D. M. Ford (Cambridge, Mass., Harvard University Press, 1940), Canto IV, verse 74, p. 139.

20. Marco Polo, *La description du monde,* ed. Louis Hambis (Klincksieck, 1955); *The Most Noble and Famous Travels of Marco Polo Together with the Travels of Nicolò de' Conti,* ed. N. M. Penzer from the Elizabethan translation of John Frampton (London, The Argonaut Press, 1929); Sir John Mandeville, *Travels,* ed. Malcolm Letts (London, Hakluyt Society, 1953).

21. René Gonnard, *La légende du bon sauvage; contribution à l'étude des origines du socialisme* (Paris, Librairie de Médicis, 1946), pp. 8–9.

22. Henri Baudet, *Onderzoekingen over het systeem der middeleeuwsche geschiedbeschouwing* (Leiden, 1948), p. 121 and bibliography; Johannus Leo Africanus, [*Navigazzioni*] *The History and Description of Africa,* trans. John Pory (London, Hakluyt Society, 1896), pp. 974 ff.

23. Harold V. Livermore, *A History of Portugal* (Cambridge, Eng., University Press, 1947), p. 185.

24. Ibid., pp. 220–21.

25. Otto von Freising, *Chronicon* (Hannoverae et Lipsiae, Monumentis Germaniae historicis, 1912), *7, 33;* cf. Isaiah 60:6.

26. J. J. Mak, *Middeleeuwse kerstvoorstellingen* (Utrecht, Spectrum, 1948); Emile Mâle, *L'art religieux en France* (Paris, Colin, 1902–08), p. 215 [Dora Nussey, *Religious Art in France* (London, Dent, 1913), p. 180]; Hugo L. Kehrer, *Die heiligen drei Könige in Litteratur und Kunst* (Leipzig, Seamann, 1908–09), *2,* 224 ff.; Karl Künstle, *Ikonographie der christlichen Kunst* (Freiberg, Herder, 1926–28), *1,* 354.

27. Jacobus de Voragine, *Legenda aurea* (Nuremberg, Koberger, 1478), Chaps. 10 and 14 [*The Golden Legend* (London, Holbein Society, 1878)].

28. Genesis 9:25.

29. Pierre d'Ailly, *Imago Mundi* [E. F. Keiner, *Imago Mundi* (Wilmington, N.C., 1948)], Chaps. 14 and 37.

30. Livermore, *History of Portugal,* p. 229. Edgar Prestage, *The Portuguese Pioneers* (London, Black, 1933).

31. D'Ailly, *Imago Mundi,* Introduction.

32. Azurara referred to it as early as 1448—*Chronicon of the Discovery and Conquest of Guinea*—and cites it in his political observations.

33. Hakluyt Society edition, *2*, 65–70.

34. See note 22, and *Europeans in West Africa 1450–1560*, ed. John W. Blake (London, Hakluyt Society, 1942).

35. Livermore, *History of Portugal*, p. 221.

36. It makes no difference, of course, that ethnology was later to differentiate between the Ethiopian and the Negro.

37. See Eva G. R. Taylor, *The Haven-Finding Art* (New York, Abelard-Schuman, 1956), pp. 154 ff.

38. Livermore, *History of Portugal*, p. 189.

39. Azurara, *Discovery of Guinea*, Chap. 7.

40. In 1434, after the conquest of Ceuta in 1415 and the expeditions to the islands between 1419 and 1433, the Portuguese began their systematic exploration of the west coast of Africa.

41. Nicolò de' Conti, pp. 145 ff.

42. See Samuel Eliot Morison, *Christopher Columbus, Mariner* (Boston, Little, Brown, 1955), p. 209 f.

43. "The discoveries were as practical in their motives as the steam-engine." R. H. Tawney, *Religion and the Rise of Capitalism* (London, Pelican Books, 1938), p. 79.

44. Gilbert Chinard, *L'exotisme Américain dans la littérature française au XVIe siècle* (Paris, Hachette, 1911), p. 7; E. Durkheim, *Les formes élémentaires de la vie religieuse* (Paris, Alcan, 1925), p. 70 [J. W. Swain, *The Elementary Forms of Religious Life* (New York, Macmillan, 1954)].

45. Pietro Martyr d'Anghiera, *De orbe novo 1511–1530* (Basel, 1533) [F. A. MacNott, *De Orbe Novo, the Eight Decades of Peter Martyr d'Anghera* (New York, G. P. Putnam's Sons, 1912)].

46. Cf. the celebrated letter dated May 1, 1500, in which Pero Vaz de Caminha reports the discovery of Brazil to King Emanuel, "Carta em que dá noticia a El Rei D. Manuel do Achamento da Terra do Brasil" in *As grandes viagens Portuguesas*, Sér. I, Selecčao, pref. e notas de Braquinho da Fonseca (Lisbon, 1948). Cf. Columbus' "Letter on His First Voyage" (Morison, *Christopher Columbus*, pp. 205–13) and Bartolomé de las Casas, *Oeuvres*, ed. J. A. Llorente (Paris, Eyemery, 1822), Introduction, pp. 7–8; Juan Ginés de Sepúlveda, "De Hispanorum rebus gestis ad novam orbem," *Opera* (Matriti, Gazeta, 1780).

47. Francis Godwin, *The Man in the Moon or a Discourse of a Voyage Thither by Domingo Gonzales* [pseud.] (1599).

48. First published in 1656 and 1662 respectively.

49. *Essays* (1580), III, 6.

50. And on Jeronimo Osorio, *De rebus Emanuelis gestis* (Olysippone, apud A. Gondisaluŭ typographum, 1571). See Gonnard, *La légende du bon sauvage,* p. 44.

51. Louis A. de Bougainville, *Voyage autour du monde* (Paris, Saillant & Nyon, 1771) [John R. Foster (London, printed for J. Nourse, 1772)].

52. Azurara, *Guinea,* Chaps. 12 and 16.

53. Ibid.

54. Las Casas, *Oeuvres,* Chap. 2, p. 24.

55. Melville J. Herskovits, *The Myth of the Negro Past* (London, Harper, 1941).

56. But in the remarkable text of Isaiah 1:18 red and white are presented as the irreconcilable, absolute opposites: "Though your sins be as scarlet, they shall be as white as snow; though they be red like crimson, they shall be as wool."

57. Las Casas, *Oeuvres,* Chap. 1, pp. 87 ff., 336 ff.; Chap. 2, pp. 205 ff. See also Henri Grégoire's celebrated speech delivered before the Institute (Paris) on May 13, 1801.

58. Guiseppe Cocchiara, *Il mito del buon selvaggio: Introduzione alla storia delle teorie ethnologiche* (Messina, D'Anna, 1948).

59. See note 17.

60. Abel Lefranc, *Les navigations de Pantagruel* (Paris, Leclerc, 1905). Rabelais, *Pantagruel, 2,* Chaps. 23–24; *Gargantua,* Chap. 56. Rabelais made extensive use of Pietro Martyr. See also Chinard, *L'exotisme Américain,* p. 49.

61. Pedro de Magelhanes de Vandavo, *Historia de provincia de Santa Cruz* (Lisbon, 1576).

62. Jean de Léry, *Histoire d'un voyage fait en la terre du Brésil, autrement dite Amérique* (Geneva, Antoine Chuppin, 1578).

63. Gilbert Chinard, *L'Amérique et le rêve exotique dans la littérature française au XVIIe et au XVIIIe siècle* (Paris, Hachette, 1913).

64. Ibid., p. 70.

65. Ibid., p. 134.

66. Henri Baudet, "Het voorspellen van historische ontwikkelingen," *Statistica* (1953), p. 206.

67. Jean Jacques Rousseau, *Discours sur l'origine et les fondements de l'inégalité* (1755), and *Du contrat social* (1762). But Rousseau later reached an entirely different conclusion. See Hoxie

N. Fairchild, *The Noble Savage: a Study in Romantic Naturalism* (New York, Columbia University Press, 1928), p. 137.

68. For example, *Le Mondain*, cited by Bury, *Idea of Progress*, p. 151.

69. Ferdinand Brunetière, *Histoire de la littérature française classique* (4 vols. Paris, Delagrave, 1904–17), *4*, 382 ff.

70. Baron de la Hontan, *Dialogue curieux entre l'auteur et un sauvage de bon sens* (1703).

71. Chinard, *Rêve exotique*, p. 230; cf. A. O. Lovejoy, "The Supposed Primitivism of Rousseau's Discourse on Inequality," *Modern Philology, 21* (1923), 165 ff.

72. Bernard de Fontenelle, *Digression sur les Anciens et les Modernes* (1688), ed. Robert Shackleton (Oxford, Clarendon Press, 1955).

73. A. M. J. Turgot, *Oeuvres* (2 vols. Paris, Guillaumin, 1844), *2*, 591–95 and 601–02.

74. Marie J. Condorcet, *Vie de Turgot* (London, 1786), pp. 273 ff. [*The Life of M. Turgot* (London, 1787), pp. 277 ff.].

75. Bury, *Idea of Progress*, p. 151.

76. See H. Taine, *Histoire de la littérature anglaise* (Paris, 1866), *4*, 83 ff. and especially 91–98 [H. Van Laun, *History of English Literature* (New York, Holt & Williams, 1872), *2*, 73 and especially 151–58]. See also W. H. Staverman, *Robinson Crusoe in Nederland* (Groningen, Modewaal, 1907), with special reference in the bibliography to the Crusoe cult in German literature.

77. For example, Gustav Klemm, *Allgemeine Cultur-Geschichte der Menschheit* (Leipzig, Teubner, 1843–52): savageness, tameness, liberty. Cf. A. Pitt-Rivers, *The Evolution of Culture* (Oxford, Clarendon Press, 1906), and R. H. Lowie, *History of Ethnological Theory*, p. 12.

78. Paul Hazard, *La crise de la conscience européenne* (3 vols. Paris, Boivin, 1939), *1*, 10 ff.

79. *Mémoires concernant l'histoire, les sciences, les arts, les moeurs, les usages, &c. des Chinois: par les missionnaires de Pékin* (16 vols. Paris, Nyon, 1776–1814). Cf. Henri Cordier, *La Chine en France au XVIIIe siècle* (Paris, Laurens, 1910); A. Reichwein, *China und Europa: Geistliche und Künstlerische Beziehungen im 18. Jahrhundert* [J. C. Powell, *China and Europe: Intellectual and Artistic Contacts in the Eighteenth Century* (New York, Knopf, 1925)]; Henri Baudet, *Katastrophe der expansie* (Indonesia, 1951), p. 128.

80. G. le Gentil, *Les Portuguais en extrême Orient; Fernão Mendes Pinto, un précurseur de l'exotisme au XVIe siècle* (Paris, Hermann, 1947), p. 321; Pyrard de Laval, *Voyage* (Paris, 1615), *1*, 331, and *4*, 101; Sir Albert Gray, ed., *The Voyage of François Pyrard of Laval* (London, Hakluyt Society, 1887–90).

81. Henri Baudet, *Eenige beschouwingen over de fransche koloniale zin en tegenzin* (Indonesia, 1953), p. 25.

82. Hazard, *La crise de la conscience européenne, 1*, 22.

83. Ibid., *1*, 24. Sir Jean Chardin, *Journal du voyage du Chevalier Chardin en Perse & aux Indes Orientales, par la Mer Noire & par la Colchide* (Londres, 1686) [Sir John Chardin's *Travels in Persia* (London, 1720)], the book which so deeply influenced Montesquieu's *Esprit des Lois*, Preface to Vol. 14 and Vol. 8, p. 21; and, of course, *Lettres Persanes*.

84. Antoine Galland, *Paroles remarquables, les bons mots et les maximes des Orientaux* (Paris, La Haye, Van Dole, 1694) [*The remarkable sayings, apothegms and maxims of the Eastern nations* (London, Printed for R. Baldwin and W. Lindsey, 1695)]; Henri de Boulainvilliers, *Vie de Mahomed* (London; Amsterdam, Humbert, 1730) [*The Life of Mohamet* (London, Printed for W. Hinchliffe, 1731)], and *Histoire des Arabes* (Amsterdam, Humbert, 1731). Antoine Galland's translation of *The Arabian Nights* appeared between 1704 and 1717. Garnier published a new edition of Claude Savary's translation of the Koran in 1948.

85. Friedrich von Schiller, *Die Verschwörung des Fiesko zu Genua*, Act III, scene 4 ["Fiesco; or, the Genoese Conspiracy" in *Schiller's Complete Works,* ed. C. Hempel (2 vols. Philadelphia, Kohler, 1861), *1*, 224].

85a. Nijkerk, Callenbach, 1956.

86. Chardin, *Journal du voyage, 4*, 101.

87. François Bernier, *Voyages* (Amsterdam, Marret, 1699), *1*, 17 [I. Brock, *Travels in the Mogul Empire* (London, W. Pickering, 1826)]; cf. Penrose, *Travel and Discovery*, pp. 79 ff. See also Henry Vignaud, *La lettre et la carte de Toscanelli sur la route des Indes par l'ouest* (Paris, Leroux, 1901), and *Histoire critique de la grande entreprise de Christophe Colomb* (Paris, Welter, 1911).

88. M. Lescarbot, *Histoire de la Nouvelle France* (Paris, 1609). Cf. Chinard, *L'Amérique*, p. 11.

89. Raynal, cited by Chinard, *Rêve exotique*, p. 395 and pp. 234 ff.

90. Chinard, *Rêve exotique*, pp. 234–35.

83

91. Cf. Johan Huizinga, "Natuurbeeld en historiebeeld in de 18e eeuw" (1933), *Verzamelde Werken, 4,* 341 ff., especially 357.

92. Jakob Burckhardt, *Weltgeschichtliche Betrachtungen* (Leipzig, Kröner, 1934), p. 8 [M. D. H., *Reflections on History* (London, Allen & Unwin, 1943), p. 18].

93. Jakob Burckhardt, *Griechische Kulturgeschichte* (Berlin, Rutten & Loening, 1955–56), *1,* 295–96 [Palmer Hilty, *History of Greek Culture* (New York, Ungar, 1963), p. 121].

94. Ibid., *1,* 239.

95. Ibid., *1,* 297 [*History of Greek Culture,* p. 122], and Strabo, *7, 5, 7.*

96. The Islamic world idealized the primitive Bedouins in this way. See, for instance, Ibn Khaldoun, *Histoire des Berbères et des dynasties musulmanes de l'Afrique septentrionale* (Alger, Imprimerie du governement, 1847–51). Cf. R. A. J. van Lier, *Sociale beweging in transculturatie* (The Hague, Nijhoff, 1956).

97. Jean-Paul Marat, *Éloge de Montesquieu* (1785); Denis Diderot, *Supplément au voyage de Bougainville* (Paris, E. Droz; Baltimore, Johns Hopkins Press, 1935). Cf. Bury, *Idea of Progress,* pp. 184–85.

98. Bury, *Idea of Progress,* p. 243.

99. Eliade, *Mythes, rêves, mystères,* pp. 37–38.

100. Thomas Salmon, *Modern History; or the Present State of All Nations* (London, Printed for Messrs. Bettesworth and Hitch, 1739), and, of course, Voltaire, Herder, etc. See also A. O. Lovejoy, *Essays in the History of Ideas* (Baltimore, Johns Hopkins Press, 1948), pp. 166 ff.

100a. Burckhardt, *Weltgeschichtliche Betrachtungen,* pp. 128 and 4 [*Reflections on History,* pp. 110 and 15].

101. Augustin Thierry, *Lettres sur l'histoire de France; dix ans d'études historiques* (Paris, Garnier, 1856), p. 80.

102. Ibid., p. 151.

103. Thierry, *Histoire de la conquête de l'Angleterre par les Normands* (1856), *1,* 7 [*History of the Conquest of England by the Normans* (New York, Dutton, 1907)].

104. Thierry, *Récits des temps mérovingiens* (ed. 1856), *2,* 82.

105. Ibid., *2,* 172.

106. J. Michelet, *Le peuple* (1841), ed. Lucien Refort (Paris, Didier, 1956), p. xxxv; [C. Cocks, *The People* (London, Longman, Brown, Green, and Longmans, 1846), p. 13].

107. Ibid., p. 103 [*The People,* p. 72].

108. Pieter Geyl, *From Ranke to Toynbee: Five Lectures on Historians and Historiographical Problems* (Northampton, Mass., Smith College, 1952), p. 27.

109. J. W. Smit, *Fruin en de partijen tijdens de Republiek* (Groningen, 1958), p. 196.

110. Geyl, *From Ranke to Toynbee*, p. 12.

111. J. Michelet, *Notre France* (Paris, Colin, 1903), pp. 290 ff.

112. Geyl, *From Ranke to Toynbee*, p. 25.

113. Gonnard, *La légende du bon sauvage*, p. 121.

114. Henri Baudet, "Geschiedenis der Wereldtentoonstellingen," *De Onderneming*, Nos. 8–12 (1958).

115. Geyl, *Encounters in History*.

116. Denis W. Brogan, *The Price of Revolution* (London, Hamilton, 1951), p. 2.

117. Daniel Halévy, *Histoire d'une histoire* (Paris, Grasset, 1939).

118. Even though South America had no European majority and the new republics were "aristocrat republics." The year 1776, that of the American Revolution, and not 1789, was deliberately selected as an example because 1776 did not abolish slavery. See Salvador de Madariaga, *The Fall of the Spanish American Empire* (London, Hollis and Carter, 1947). I have had frequent recourse to his biographies of Columbus, Cortes, etc.

119. Paul Valéry, *Variété* (Paris, Nouvelle Revue Française, 1924), p. 49 [Malcolm Cowley, *Variety* (New York, Harcourt, Brace, 1927), p. 52].

120. Ernest A. Seillière, *Pour le centenaire du romantisme* (Paris, Champion, 1927), pp. 97–127.

121. Etienne de Sénancour, *Rêveries sur la nature primitive de l'homme* (Paris, Champion, 1799).

122. Raoul Allier, *Le non-civilisé et nous* (Paris, Payot, 1927), p. 26 [Fred Rothwell, *The Mind of the Savage* (New York, Harcourt, Brace, 1929), p. 19].

123. This word is to be found as a sort of personal motto in all of Seillière's works.

124. David O. Evans, *Social Romanticism in France* (Oxford, Clarendon Press, 1951).

125. Ernest Renan, quoted by Allier, *Le non-civilisé*, p. 19, although his reference to *Questions contemporaines* on p. 35 does not tally.

126. Baudet, *Katastrophe*, p. 125.

127. Baudet, *Zin en tegenzin,* p. 32.

128. Hans Plischke, *Von Cooper bis Karl May* (Düsseldorf, Droste, 1951). Jules Verne's Aouda, like Winnetou, is a highly exceptional case. But it should be borne in mind that she had received a Western education. See *Journey Around the World in Eighty Days.*

129. A good indication is provided by Joseph L. A. Calmette, *Les révolutions* (Paris, Fayard, 1952), pp. 730 ff. "On the 12th of July 1870, *Le Réveil,* organ of the Paris internationals, published 'an appeal to our German brothers.' Karl Marx undertook to reply. On the 20th he wrote to Engels, 'The French need a thrashing . . . If the Prussians win, the centralization of the power of the state will be useful in the centralization of the German working class. Besides, German preponderance will move the center of gravity of the European workers' movement from France to Germany. The preponderance, on the world scene, of the German proletariat over the French proletariat would be, at the same time, the preponderance of our theory over that of Proudhon.' " (Karl Marx and Friedrich Engels, *Briefwechsel, 9* [Berlin, Marx-Engels-Verlag, 1931], 339). Also quoted by Édouard Dolléans, *Féminisme et le mouvement ouvrier* (Paris, Les Editions Ouvrières, 1958), p. 337.

130. *Cecil Rhodes: a Biography and Appreciation by Imperialist. With Personal Reminiscences by Dr. Jameson* (London, Chapman & Hall, 1897), p. 404. See also Vindex [pseud.], *Cecil Rhodes: his Political Life and Speeches 1881–1900* (London, Chapman & Hall, 1900). But Rhodes regarded the European as the natural and absolute superior of the "yellow" and, more specifically, the "black" races. Cf. Seillière, *Introduction,* p. 65.

131. Baudet, *Zin en tegenzin,* p. 33.

132. H. M. Stanley, *How I Found Livingstone* (New York, Scribner, Armstrong; Boston, Smith, 1872), p. 234; Albert Maurice, ed., *H. M. Stanley: Unpublished Letters* (London, Chambers, 1955).

133. Ernest Renan, *Caliban,* Act I, scene 1 (Paris, Calmann Lévy, 1878) [E. G. Vickery (New York, The Shakespeare Press; London, K. Paul Trench, Trubner, 1896)].

134. See Henriëtte de Beaufort, *Cornelis van Vollenhoven* (Haarlem, H. D. Tjeenk Willink, 1954), pp. 15–18. "Renan who, without prejudice, tried to understand both belief and disbelief in the history of the development of mankind." See also Jules Har-

mand, *Dominaton et colonisation* (Paris, Flammarion, 1910), and Paul Leroy-Beaulieu, *De la colonisation chez les peuples modernes* (6th ed. Paris, Alcan, 1908).

135. Burckhardt, *Weltgeschichtliche Betrachtungen,* pp. 128, 134 [*Reflections on History,* p. 110].

136. In addition to Brogan's *Price of Revolution* see Bernard Groethuysen, *Philosophie de la révolution française; précédé de Montesquieu* (4th ed. Paris, Gallimard, 1956), pp. 289 ff.

137. Ernest Renan, *L'eau de Jouvence, suite de Caliban* (Paris, 1880), Act V, scene 3.

138. I wish to draw attention to Fritz Kern's profound little book, *Der Beginn der Weltgeschichte* (Berne, Francke, 1953), an examination of the basic principles of natural law, and a great deal more besides.